Sermons from the Heart in Trying Times

Steve Starzer

Parson's Porch Books

Sermons from the Heart in Trying Times

ISBN: Softcover 978-1-951472-95-5

Copyright © 2021 by Steve Starzer

All rights reserved. No part of this book may be reproduced or transmitted in any form or by any means, electronic or mechanical, including photocopying, recording, or by any information storage and retrieval system, without permission in writing from the publisher.

Parson's Porch Books is an imprint of Parson's Porch *&* Company (PP*&*C) in Cleveland, Tennessee. PP*&*C is an innovative organization which raises money by publishing books of noted authors, representing all genres. Its face and voice is **David Russell Tullock** (dtullock@parsonsporch.com).

Sermons from the Heart in Trying Times

Contents

Acknowledgements	8
Foreword	12
Introduction	14
Who Do You Say That I Am?	16
Matthew 17: 1-9	
If Christ Were Not Raised	20
Matthew 28, 1-10, 16-20	
Boot Camp for the Soul	25
John 4: 5-42	
Easter Means Hope	30
Matthew 28: 1 - 10	
Walking with Jesus	35
Luke 24: 13-35	
Personal Relationships	41
John 14: 1- 14	
Knowing God by Name	45
Acts 17: 22-31	
Hurry Up and Wait	50
Acts 1: 6-14	
Sheltering in Place	56
Acts 2: 1-13	
Holy Trinity with Us	61
Matthew 28: 16-20	
Never Abandoned	65
Genesis 21: 8-21	
God Will Provide?	70
Genesis 22: 1-14	
Designing Love	75
Genesis 24: 34-38, 42-49, 58-67	
Broken Spirits, Broken Bodies	81
Romans 8: 1-14	

Labor Pains 86
    Romans 8: 12 - 25

Inseparable 91
    Romans 8: 26 - 39

Not the Normal Way 97
    Romans 9: 1-5

The Math of Forgiveness 102
    Matthew 18: 21-35

A Fair Wage 108
    Matthew 20: 1-16

Nostalgia 114
    Exodus 17: 1 - 7

Worry 120
    Philippians 4:1-9

Greed 124
    Matthew 22: 15-22

Disappointment 130
    Deuteronomy 34: 1-12

The Other Side of the Curtain 136
    Revelation 7: 9 - 17

Grieving with Hope 142
    I Thessalonians 4: 13-18

How Many Shopping Days Left? 147
    Psalm 90: 1-12

The End of the World as We Know It 152
    Mark 13: 24-37

Where the Wild Things Are 157
    Isaiah 40: 1-11

Pitching the Tent 161
    2nd Samuel 7: 1-11, 16

Counting Your Blessings 165
    Ephesians 1: 3 – 14

God Created 171
    Genesis 1: 1-5

Creating Christian Freedom 177
    I Corinthians 6: 12 – 20

Never-Ending Creativity 183
    Isaiah 40: 21 – 31

Descending to Share the Story 191
    Mark 9: 2-9

Change 195
    Mark 1: 9-15

Go into All The World 201
    Philemon 1-22

Basic Construction 204
    1 Corinthians 3: 1-17

The Midnight Wedding 210
    Matthew 25:1-13 (NLT)

Acknowledgements

I owe so many people so much gratitude that it is almost impossible to think about how to list every single one on a piece of paper. Of course I need to begin with my family. I am deeply blessed because of my family. There isn't a chance in the world that I would have made it through 40 years of ministry without my beautiful wife, Debby. She has been a constant source of support, joy and deep friendship for 36 years. Courtney Anne, my eldest child, and her husband, Miheer, have moved closer to us and that brings me a great deal of happiness. Chad, who has entered the other family business as a Firefighter/Medic with Hanover Fire/EMS, brings me great pride. I love each of you dearly and deeply.

My oldest brother, Paul, gave me a hard time because I didn't mention him or my sister, Miriam Baker, in my last book. It wasn't because I don't love them. In their own ways each has been a support to me in my life. It was Miriam, who before I was ordained bought me a classic reference volume to start my pastoral library. It is Paul who challenges me to live up to the standards our Father set. Thank you both for being my siblings. Our late brother, John, was always a support to me in subtle ways. He would come and listen to my sermons and he was an anonymous donor to my congregations, which he accidentally let slip to me once. John is missed deeply by all of his family.

I have been privileged to work with some very fine colleagues over the years. Each of them has brought something special to my life and I am deeply appreciative for each one of them. I can't mention them all but let me say that the two I worked most closely with were Robert Peak and Steve Chastain. Robert Peak and Steve Chastain remind me of a character I read in a novel, who had tremendous gifts and abilities but never sought honor or distinction but rather sought to minister faithfully in places where few would notice. Both Steve and Robert have spent the majority of their lives serving humbly and well in congregations others would have walked away from but their faithfulness has touched countless lives with the love of Jesus Christ. They will always have my love and admiration.

The good people I work with right now are incredible. Roy W. Jones, early in my ministry said, "Surround yourself with good people and then stay out of their way. " That was sage advice that has proved true here at Fairfield Presbyterian Church. The two closest to me on a daily basis are my colleague, Darren Utley and our extraordinary church secretary, Donna Carson. Darren has made my ministry a lot easier and a lot more fun. His good work is exceeded only by his wonderful sense of humor. He has made difficult days a lot lighter and I am thankful. Donna has made Darren's and my work so much easier and so much more efficient. She never calls attention to herself and not only works tirelessly to accomplish all of her myriad responsibilities but always makes everyone feel loved and welcomed. Darren and I have joked that if she ever resigns our letters of resignation would quickly follow hers because we know we would be lost without her.

My "other job" as a Chaplain with Hanover Fire/EMS has brought me many wonderful experiences and introduced me to some of the finest and bravest people I have ever known. They welcomed me in as if I had always been a part of their family. From firefighters to lieutenants to battalion chiefs to Assistant Chief Chris Anderson, my boss, to our Chief Jethro Piland III, to my fellow chaplains, Chris Miller, Will Pannell and retired Chief Mike Harman, Sr. , I count them one and all as friends. I have gained more from them than I have given and I am deeply grateful.

The number of people I could thank for helping me to be the person that I am is innumerable. It would be easier to write a book of just naming everyone and telling why they have been so important to me. To all those who remain unnamed here, please know that your names are close to my heart and I am blessed to have you in my life.

When it is all said and done, I am grateful to God. It is only by the Grace of God that a gangly teenage boy who was shyer than shy would be called to be a Pastor/Preacher. By every standard of measurement, I was the wrong person to go into ministry. Yet, here

I am at forty years in looking back on three wonderful pastorates and looking forward to more years here at Fairfield. I often joke when complimented on a sermon that I have a Holy Ghost writer. But as I look back on my life and ministry, I don't think I was wrong. Thanks be to God and to God alone be all glory and honor.

In Christ's love,

Steve

Foreword

Like so many others, I love a trip to the beach. I find both refreshment and renewal when I am there mesmerized by the waves and salt air. It is the place in nature I feel closest to God. However as much as I love that setting, I am somewhat hesitant to wade into waters beyond being able to see my feet. There seems to be an element of danger of stepping on a sharp shell, sands shifting underfoot, or even stepping into an unseen hole. I always felt steadier when my husband would walk beside me with his hand at my elbow giving me encouragement to wade a little further out.

As an adult I have approached scripture in much the same way. I love Bible study and return again and again to the words that refresh, encourage, and bring me closer to God. But there also are passages that can pierce my conscious like a sharp shell. Learning that passages I have interpreted through my 21st century understanding have a totally different meaning within the context of the time in which they were written feels like shifting sands. When I encounter the anger of God in the Old Testament it feels like the unsure footing of stepping into a hole. I have found through Steve's sermons, Bible studies, and even my direct questions that his approach is much like a steadying hand on my elbow, encouraging me to look deeper and continue to explore and learn from even those uncomfortable passages.

Without doubt, Steve's sermon that I hold most dear was from my husband's funeral. While I knew the words chosen with care would be a comfort to our grieving family, I was not expecting and surprised by the reactions of many of the others who attended. For days and even weeks afterward, friends who had known Rick from his childhood neighborhood, school classmates, college fraternity brothers, work colleagues from a 32-year career told me over and over how that funeral sermon so resonated with them and their own relationship with Rick. These connections and friendships came from very different points in Rick's over six decades of life. I still find that astonishing.

I probably should have not been surprised because I often find Steve's sermons to be almost directed personally to me. I frequently feel very connected to his words and there have been many times that others in our congregation have commented that his sermon was exactly what they needed to hear that day. As you read through these sermons and the stories that Steve weaves within them, you may find one or two that appear to have your name on them. You may find yourself thinking, "This sermon was written especially for me."If so, I can assure you, indeed it was!

Martha Houchins, Elder
Fairfield Presbyterian Church

Introduction

"Take your Bible and take your newspaper, and read both. But interpret newspapers from your Bible." Karl Barth. This is an often misquoted statement. The distinction Barth was trying to make and is often missed in the misquote is that the Scripture shed light on our lives and in the times in which we find ourselves living. It has also been stated that the role of the preacher is to bring timeless truth in a timely manner.

No matter how you say it, the role of the Pastor/Preacher is to offer a Biblical perspective that helps his/her congregation to fully celebrate good times and to faithfully endure challenging times. The year 2020 will always be remembered as one of the most challenging years we have endured in recent history. Covid-19 and the political unrest were dueling for our attention and each in their own way has attempted to shape our lives and not necessarily for the better. The majority of the sermons found in this volume are ones which were preached to the good people of Fairfield Presbyterian (either remotely or later in person) during this trying time. We have sought to offer a strongly Biblical perspective in a manner which is both uplifting and challenging.

I need you to note that my colleague, The Rev. Darren Utley, and I have chosen to preach using the lectionary and using a themed series approach. We have generally been guided by two volumes of <u>A Preacher's Guide to Lectionary Sermon Series</u> published by Westminster John Knox. We mostly used it to guide the series and rarely followed their recommendations for the central focus of the sermons. Both Darren and I know that preaching is a very personal matter and one must be faithful to one's own style and theology when approaching the pulpit.

While this volume is one written in a particular time and context, I hope and pray that the timeless truth of the Bible will always be known to the reader in whatever time one finds one's self. This volume comes to you with my prayer that the words found on these pages will reveal to you the God of love and grace whom we know so well through the person and work of Jesus Christ.

Steve Starzer
4 March 2021
Mechanicsville, VA

Who Do You Say That I Am?
Matthew 17: 1-9

March 1, 1987

Introduction

I have always shied away from mystery novels. I don't know why. I can't give you a good reason why I have avoided reading them. My Dad has always loved them. I don't know how many thousands he has read down through the years and he has enjoyed each and every one of them. He has gotten to the point now where the big thrill for him is seeing how soon in the book he can figure out "who done it."I did read the very first one in my life this past Christmas. I read it for two different reasons. First, it was a gift and at that it was a gift from my mother-in-law, so common sense told me it would be beneficial to read it. The second reason was because the hero-detective of the novel was a minister and I am always willing to read something which has a positive portrayal of the clergy.

Now, to be honest with you, I don't have the skill in reading mystery novels that my father has. I got tricked by every little clue the author threw at me. If I had been the detective-clergyman I would have condemned the wrong person time and time again. It would be obvious to you then that unlike my Dad the part which I enjoyed the most was the very end. I didn't have any idea what was going on until the preacher turned detective gathered all of the suspects together in the final scene of the book. He drew all of the pieces of the puzzle together than all of a sudden it made a great deal of sense to me. What a revelation!

I

For the twelve disciples there was a certain mystery evolving. They had been traveling together for three years now and they were convinced that this Jesus of Nazareth was somebody quite unique: a person unlike anyone they had ever known before. But they couldn't quite put their finger on what it was about this man that made him so different. Was it the miracles he worked? No, it wasn't quite that - there had been plenty of miracle workers and magicians before Jesus came along. Was it the fact that he could teach a lesson or tell a story so well? No, it wasn't quite that either. There were plenty of other Rabbis who could be spell binding in their presentations and creative in their thought. There was something about this man Jesus and the authority with which he spoke and acted that caused them to follow him without question. After all, this is the one who drew them away from their families, their livelihoods and home towns to wander through the countryside. There was definitely something about this man which was unlike anyone whom they had ever met before. Much like the mystery novel, they knew all of the pieces were there but they just couldn't see how the whole picture fell together.

II

I think we need to take a look to see how this puzzle was falling together for the disciples of Jesus. They had spent the better part of three years together. They had seen so many different kinds of things it would make your head spin. They watched as demons were cast out, they watched as the outcasts were welcomed, they saw the lame, the blind and the dying being held, they heard a preacher teach with a fervor they had never known before and they watched in amazement as the crowds came and grew to the point where there was literally thousands upon the hillside. It wasn't as if anyone really understood this man but they were all agreed that there was something very special about him. He was someone worth listening to. For those who were closest to him they were also the closest to the solution of this mystery of what was so special about this man from Nazareth. As a matter of fact just a little while before the incident in this morning's scripture lesson, Jesus put the question to his disciples, "Who do you say that I am? "It was Peter, one of the closest to Jesus, who came up with the right answer, "You are the Christ, the son of the living God. "

Peter had the answer right there before him. It came rolling off his lips as easily as any answer he had ever given before. But like the people in the mystery novel, the obvious answer is often times the most difficult to understand. Even after he mentally was able to say, "you are the Christ, the son of the living God," it would take a mountain top experience to drive home the reality of the truth of his confession of faith.

III

From that mountain top three of the disciples - Peter, James and James' brother John - saw the full picture of who Jesus is in a way that changed their whole lives. There upon the mountain top all of the principles of the mystery were gathered. For not only was Jesus there but also Elijah and Moses - the prophet and the patriarch. All of the history of God's work for our salvation came together in that time and in that place. And the mighty hand of God was placed upon Jesus and he was glorified. It was a sight like nothing else they had ever seen or ever would see on this earth again. They responded the same as you and I would: they were scared half to death. What they saw was the face of Jesus shining as bright as the sun and his clothes were as bright as the noon day light! And if that weren't enough suddenly a bright cloud surrounded them and a voice rang out with power and authority, "This is my Son, whom I love; with him I am well pleased. Listen to him! "

The mystery was solved. The great solver of all mysteries gathered them together much like the author of the novel did and he revealed the truth. For these disciples this moment was one which changed their whole lives. For in that moment they realized the fact that God

Himself is with us! What was so special about this man? In his humanness there was God! All of the preachers, teachers, prophets, presidents and world leaders can never claim that. There is only one of whom it is said, "the Word became flesh and dwelt among us."

Conclusion

For those few disciples, the reality that Jesus Christ is the Son of God changed their very existence. For you and me the claims of the one who is the son of God still touch us the same as they touched Peter, James and John some two-thousand years ago. On that mountain top it was not only Jesus who was changed but the disciples as well. In this valley where we live, work and worship, it is we who need to be transfigured: it is we who come face to face with the living God through his Son Jesus Christ. And when we truly come face to face with him we cannot walk away unchanged!

If Christ Were Not Raised
Matthew 28, 1-10, 16-20

April 15, 1990

In the 28th chapter of Matthew, we'll read verses 1-10 and then 16-20.

After the Sabbath, at dawn on the first day of the week, Mary Magdalene and the other Mary went to look at the tomb. There was a violent earthquake, for an angel of the Lord came down from heaven and, going to the tomb, rolled back the stone and sat on it. His appearance was like lightning, and his clothes were white as snow. The guards were so afraid of him that they shook and became like dead men. The angel said to the women, "Do not be afraid, for I know that you are looking for Jesus, who was crucified. He is not here; he has risen, just as he said. Come and see the place where he lay. Then go quickly and tell his disciples: 'He has risen from the dead and is going ahead of you into Galilee. There you will see him. Now I have told you. "So the women hurried away from the tomb, afraid yet filled with joy, and ran to tell his disciples. Suddenly Jesus met them. "Greetings," he said. They came to him, clasped his feet and worshiped him. Then Jesus said to them, "Do not be afraid. Go and tell my brothers to go to Galilee; there they will see me."

Then the eleven disciples went to Galilee to the mountain where Jesus had told them to go. When they saw him, they worshiped him; but some doubted. Then Jesus came to them and said, "All authority in heaven and on earth has been given to me. Therefore go and make disciples of all nations, baptizing them in the name of the Father and of the Son and of the Holy Spirit, and teaching them to obey everything I have commanded you. And surely I am with you always, to the very end of the age. May the Lord bless this a portion from his holy word.

One of my favorite movies is actually a Christmas movie. It's called "It a Wonderful Life."It's an older film starring Jimmy Stewart and it raises an interesting proposition. In this movie, for all of you who are familiar with it, you know that the hero of the movie is going through some very hard times. In his despair, he cries out that he wished he'd never been born! But his guardian angel is with him and grants him his wish. So the hero of the movie has that opportunity to see what life would have been like had he not lived. The movie goes on to show what a positive effect the hero's life had upon so many different people.

There was a novel that was written a number of years ago, quite a number of years ago actually, and in this novel the author brings up the question, a similar question but this time the question is not about some imaginary figure, the question is raised about Jesus Christ. What would happen if Jesus Christ had not been raised from the dead? My friends, that's an interesting question, isn't it? What would this world today be like if Jesus Christ had never been raised from the dead? What would our world look like today if Jesus was not alive on that first Easter morning? How would things be different? Well, if we stepped back to the most obvious at the very beginning, we would realize that there would be no Christian Church. After all, we remember on Good Friday when our Lord was crucified and died, the disciples were distraught, they were in despair, they each went their own way. They didn't know what to do. Peter denied him, Judas betrayed him and all the others simply abandoned him. It took something, something extraordinary to take those people with broken dreams and shattered hopes to bring them around again. If Christ had not risen, they would have remained scattered and confused.

Take a look at Peter. Here was a man that just a few days before, when confronted among a hand full of people, denied even knowing Jesus Christ. What was it that took him from being willing to deny Christ in front of a hand full of people to be willing to proclaim Jesus Christ before thousands of people and to preach in such a positive way that thousands were persuaded to follow Jesus Christ? It had to be something large, something great, that changed Peter from one who would deny to one who would proclaim. Certainly, if Christ were not raised Peter would not have preached. Without those early disciples, without their proclamation, without their faith, the church, the Christian church would not have been born.

Think for a moment about how different the world would be today if there were no Christian churches within it. The steeples that dot the countryside, the ones that stand tall and proud within our towns, villages and cities, they would not be there to proclaim the love of God had Christ not been raised. Or, how about this land in which we live? Would America be the same today had Christ not been raised from the dead? There would have been no Puritans, no Quakers, no others who sought to serve the risen Lord in the new land. Even our Constitution itself reflects the Christian values of human dignity and human rights, that Jesus not only taught but showed us in the way that he lived his life. If Christ had not been raised we would have none of that.

What of our schools? What of our hospitals? In virtually every town, and Wyalusing is no exception, the first schools were built and staffed by the churches. The preachers were often the teachers as well. And our hospitals in many towns were founded as Christian institutions for after all, wasn't it Christ who taught us compassion? Wasn't it Christ who taught us the value of knowledge? If Christ were not raised how different would our world be?

On my desk, I have a volume that's entitled, "The Mission Yearbook of Prayer" and in this volume, it's a rather significant paperback, it outlines for us all of the different mission projects that we Presbyterians support in this land and throughout the world. It talks about churches, schools, hospitals, training centers, seminaries and the list goes on and on of all the different ways that we as a Christian church are proclaiming the love of God through word and deed. Now, if you took that book, that list of mission projects and you multiplied that list by all of the other Christian churches in the world, you would soon find that the Christian church today is touching the lives of millions of people. If Christ were not raised from the dead.

If there were no Christian church, the world would be suffering more pain, far more despair, far more hunger, disease and pestilence.

If Christ were not raised from the dead, there would have been no one who went forth making disciples of all nations and teaching us to observe all that Christ has commanded. If Christ were not raised, you and I would be living in a world filled with darkness and despair. And what of you and I personally? The scriptures tell us "If for this life only we have hope, then we of all people ought to be pitied. "If Christ were not raised from the dead, you and I would not have that hope that burns in our hearts, we would not have that hope for this life, nor would we have that hope for the life yet to come.

I have to tell you folks that one of the saddest tasks that I ever performed was the day I did a funeral for a man whose family had no church connections at all. None of them had ever been members of any church. None of them ever heard the Good News of Jesus Christ and I went in to that funeral home and I looked around and I saw the saddest faces that one could ever see. I talked with those people, I listened to them and one by one each of them told me of their pain in the fact that they would never see their loved one again. They had no hope. They had no vision of what Christ has done in the resurrection from the grave. For them, the death of a loved one was a final act, a cutting off. That person would be someone they would see never again. But, not so for us Christians. For even in the midst of the darkest moments of our lives, we have hope because Christ is risen! . Death is conquered. You and I have hope because life everlasting is ours. My friends, we could spend all day conjecturing about what it would be like if Christ were not raised but that would be all that is was, just conjecture: a moot point! . For the fact of the matter is this, Jesus Christ is alive today. If you want evidence, if you want proof, just look around you in this world today. For this world is a far better place because of Christ's death and resurrection. And even more important than that is the fact that a better world awaits us because in his resurrection, Jesus Christ has conquered death.

Jesus Christ is risen! Christ is risen indeed! And within that message lies hope for you and me. In that message lies the challenge for us to share that word of good news, for us to continually bring about change for the better in our world. As we seek to go out to make disciples, teaching them all that Christ has commanded us. My friends the proclamation is clear: Christ is risen! Christ is risen indeed! Amen.

Boot Camp for the Soul
John 4: 5-42

March 15, 2020

I've never preached before a broadcast service. I was really having a little higher expectations, I really thought that Darren would start off the service this morning by going "Live from Mechanicsville - it's Sunday morning! " but I didn't get that, so for those who are watching from the comfort of your homes and worshiping from there, we are glad you are with us! These are challenging times. These are times that raise all sorts of questions and fears in many of our hearts. But if there's any place that we need to turn to in trying times, it's to the church, to the body of Jesus Christ in this world. So, I'm glad for those of you that are here and I'm glad for those of you who are with us via the internet so that together maybe we can find some comfort, some encouragement. Maybe as someone reminded me this morning, we can find some normalcy that we are looking for in our lives in this day and age.

The passage that ironically was already chosen for today before we had all this happening with the Corona virus, is a text that deals oddly enough with isolation and separation. It's not unusual situation in the biblical times, the laws of the Old Testament were very clear about isolating those who were unclean. Those who had certain diseases, what have you, were to be separated from the community and kept away from the others. It was just one of those signs of God's wisdom to the Hebrew people that pre-dated a lot of our knowledge about contagions and so on. That tradition, that heritage of isolating those who were unclean is a part of our Judeo-Christian heritage.

But this particular story is one about a woman who is isolated because she was unclean, not because of any illness, but because of decisions that she made in her life. We'll hear her story in just a minute. But we do need to turn to the pages of scripture, we do need to turn to God in prayer, we do need to encourage one another and to be there with and for one another even if it is without the benefit of a hug or a handshake but just a simple conversation or online or however it is we might be with people. Talking about communications, my nephew sent me a text this morning with a meme in it that highlighted for us that part of Lent is we are to learn how to love like Jesus and wash our hands like Pontius Pilate. So, this is the first time in my ministry that Pontius Pilate is raised up as an example for us of his hand-washing abilities.

Let's take a look at this story. It's one that you're probably all familiar with. I'm not going to read all 37 verses that make up the whole story but let me read to you the first 26 and then I'll pick up at the 39th.

"The Pharisees heard that Jesus was gaining and baptizing more disciples than John, although, in fact is was not Jesus who baptized, but his disciples. When the Lord learned of this, he left Judea and went back once more to Galilee. Now he had to go through Samaria. So he came to a town in Samaria called Sychar, near the plot of ground Jacob had given to his son Joseph. Jacob's well was there, and Jesus, tired as he was from the journey, sat down by the well. It was about the sixth hour. When a Samaritan women came to draw water, Jesus said to her, "Will you give me a drink? "(His disciples had gone into the town to buy food.)The Samaritan woman said to him, "You are a Jew and I am a Samaritan woman. How can you ask me for a drink? " (For Jews do not associate with Samaritans.)Jesus answered her, "If you knew the gift of God and who it is that asks you for a drink, you would have asked him and he would have given you living water. ""Sir," the woman said, "you have nothing to draw with and the well is deep. Where can you get this living water? Are you greater than our father Jacob who gave us the well and drank from it himself, as did also his sons and his flocks and herds? "Jesus answered, "Everyone who drinks this water will be thirsty again, but whoever drinks the water I give him will never thirst. Indeed, the water I give him will become in him a spring of water welling up to eternal life. "The woman said to him, "Sir, give me this water so that I won't get thirsty and have to keep coming here to draw water. "He told her, "Go, call your husband and come back. ""I have no husband," she replied. Jesus said to her, "You are right when you say you have no husband. The fact is you have had five husbands, and the man you now have is not your husband. What you have just said is quite true. ""Sir," the woman said, I can see that you are a

prophet. Our fathers worshiped on this mountain, but you Jews claim that the place where we must worship is in Jerusalem. "Jesus declared, "Believe me, woman, a time is coming when you will worship the Father neither on this mountain nor in Jerusalem. You Samaritans worship what you do not know; we worship what we do know, for salvation is from the Jews. Yet a time is coming and has now come when the true worshipers will worship the Father in spirit and truth, for they are the kind of worshipers the Father seeks. God is spirit, and his worshipers must worship in spirit and in truth. "The woman said, "I know that Messiah" (called Christ) is coming. When he comes, he will explain everything to us. "Then Jesus declared, "I who speak to you am he."

And we'll pick it up in the 39th verse:

Many of the Samaritans from that town believed in him because of the woman's testimony, "He told me everything I ever did. "So when the Samaritans came to him, they urged him to stay with them, and he stayed two days. And because of his words many more became believers. They said to the woman, "We no longer believe just because of what you said; now we have heard for ourselves, and we know that this man really is the Savior of the world. 'May the Lord bless this a portion from his holy word.

This is an odd text with an odd story to tell. It is one that may be, as we read it, in this 21st century, we don't see a lot of the nuances or a lot of the issues that were taking place here. There was this conversation between Jesus and this Samaritan woman. Now, for a first century Jewish reader, it would have been a shocking thing for that reader to hear of Jesus doing this. A - she was a Samaritan. Jews hated Samaritans. Jews had no use for Samaritans because they were too close - they were Jewish but intermingled with the people of other communities and they ended up with this blended religion that was neither fish nor fowl! The Jews thought that was the worst thing ever and so the Samaritans were refuse. Secondly, she was a woman. For a man to talk to a woman he did not know or was not his own wife or sister or mother or some other close relative was an anathema- you just didn't do that. Thirdly, this woman was there in the heat of the day which tells us she was there around noon or so on that day coming to get her water from the well. The reason that she came at noon, not like all the others who would come and get their water from the well in the cool of the dawn of the new day when it was easier to carry the water and it was cooler. In the early morning hours there would be all sorts of people there and you would have conversations, you would catch up with each other and you would do the business of the day in the fellowship of that circle. But she came at noon because the pattern of her life, the decisions she made caused her to be ostracized from the community. She couldn't be a part of the conversation other than people talking about her shame.

So, this woman, this Samaritan woman at the well had three strikes against her: she was a Samaritan, she was a woman and a woman with a bad reputation of having made bad decisions. Yet Jesus still conversed with her. And Jesus offered to her the living water, the living water of Jesus' love, Jesus' grace, of the love of God, the forgiveness and the mercy of God. A water that quenches in a way that H20 never will. He offered it to this woman who was isolated, cast out, set aside from society. The interesting thing is she went back into her community and she began to talk with others about this Jesus that she had met at the well and told them her story and told them how Jesus knew everything about her and urged them to believe. And they asked Jesus to stay and be with them, teach them, talk with them and they believed in him.

Now one of the things you have to see is the fact that this woman, isolated, cast aside, a "persona non grata" to her community, now became a part of her community. These conversations that she had, this bond that she developed with the others in her community, she was so excited about what she had found in Jesus she just had to share that with all of them. Then all of a sudden she became a part of the community. She was no longer cast out. She became one that others listened to. She was appreciated because of what she had told them.

This living water that we need, this living water that Jesus offers draws us together. This gift of his love is something that if we truly understand it, if we truly appreciate it, we can't hold it in isolation from others. It forces us to be in community, it forces us to care about each other more than we even care about ourselves, it forces us to recognize that there are those whom we may have ostracized from our own lives, those whom we may have stepped aside and deemed not worthy of our time, our energy, of our compassion. And it forces us to see them as ones who are loved by God as well. This living water draws us all to the well and encourages us all to bring others to the well so that together we might enjoy that grace and love and mercy so freely given to us.

In this time of dealing with the Corona virus, hopefully not dealing with it, preventing ourselves from dealing with it might be our goal, our aspiration, we find ourselves trying to live in a certain isolation from each other. That is the way we fight this disease. But what I'm going to suggest to all of us is that while we might not enjoy the handshakes, the hugs, the large gatherings, we might not enjoy all of that during this season, let us make an extra effort to find ways to be in community. I challenge you to call somebody today, just to say, "Hi, how are you doing?" Maybe somebody you haven't talked with in a long while, maybe somebody that you might have been on the outs with or maybe somebody that you know doesn't have a lot of family and in this isolation from this disease, those who maybe are older, have pulmonary illnesses or whatever it might be that forces them to be even more isolated than others, give them a call, be in touch with them, let them know they are loved, cared for. In spite of this isolation that is forced upon us let us find ways that we can share the living water with the love of Jesus Christ - for others who are so thirsty for it. Would you pray with me?

Almighty and ever-loving God, we give you thanks for the love of Jesus Christ. A love that knows no boundary, not even a Samaritan, not even that woman is rejected by his love but is included instead and shown compassion and care. O heavenly Father, help us to walk in the ways of Jesus Christ, to love as Jesus has loved, to find community even when we live in isolation. We pray this in Jesus' name and for his sake, Amen.

Easter Means Hope
Matthew 28: 1 - 10

April 12, 2020

Let's take a look at the reason that we get together on this Sunday and the particular reason that we get together on Easter Sunday to retell, to rehear, the story of Christ's resurrection; the conquering of death for us all. So let's take a look at it from Matthew in the 28th chapter, the first 10 verses there.

*After the Sabbath, at dawn on the first day of the week, Mary Magdalene and the other Mary went to look at the tomb. There was a violent earthquake, for an angel of the Lord came down from heaven and, going to the tomb, rolled back the stone and sat on it. His appearance was like lightning, and his clothes were as white as snow. The guards were so afraid of him that they shook and became like dead men. The angel said to the women, "Do not be afraid, for I know that you are looking for Jesus, who was crucified. He is not here; he has risen, just as he said. Come and see the place where he lay. Then go quickly and tell his disciples: 'He has risen from the dead and is going ahead of you into Galilee. There you will see him.' Now I have told you. "So the women hurried away from the tomb, afraid yet filled with joy, and ran to tell his disciples. Suddenly Jesus met them. "Greetings," he said. They came to him, clasped his feet and worshiped him. Then Jesus said to them, "Do not be afraid. Go tell my brothers to go to Galilee; there they will see me. '*May the Lord bless this a very special portion of his holy word.

I had a telephone conversation this week with a colleague, a good friend of mine, and we were just talking about our situations, talking about how things were going and how things were shaping up in each of our respective congregations. Right in the middle of that conversation he says to me, "Starzer, you're obnoxious. "It's not the first time I've heard that and it won't be the last time I've heard that. But I said, "What do you mean? "He said, "Here I am telling you everything I'm worried about in my church, I'm worried about our future, I'm worried about how we're going to make ends meet, I'm worried about this, I'm worried about that and all you can talk about are the good things that are happening in your church. "I said, "Yea, I think we're going to come out of this stronger because of what we've gone through. We're doing some creative stuff. We're using technology I never thought we would ever use or even knew half of this stuff existed. I didn't know what Zoom was but fortunately Darren does! So we're in good shape because Darren understands these things that I don't understand. "And as he and I went on to talk some more, I began to realize that there were just two perspectives of the same situation. While my good friend was living in fear I'd chosen a different route. I choose to look at all of this with hope in my eyes; of looking at the good things that God is bringing out of it; the good things will help to shape us in the future.

There are so many things that I have seen happening in the life of this church in these last few weeks. There has been so many signs of love and compassion, ways that people are caring for each other, the spirit and attitude of helpfulness, the desire to do for each other has just been heartwarming for me. Even though we can't be a congregation gathering in, coming together, we can still be the church. And I have been extremely impressed, extremely touched by the way that all of you have been the church in these times. Doing the right things, doing the acts of love, showing compassion, being the church in this time, in this place, among your friends, with your families, so I've been very impressed with that and it gives me hope for the future.

And as I was thinking about this text, this great story of the resurrection, of Mary Magdalene and the other Mary who went to the grave, it's kind of interesting that it says they went to look at it. I'm not sure what that means because the other gospels talk about going there to finish preparing the body for its entombment. But, none the less, they go to the grave, they find themselves in a situation that they didn't imagine would ever happen - they find themselves coming face to face with an angel of the Lord. They find themselves coming face to face not with wondering how they were going to move the rock but finding the rock already moved. Not finding out how they were going to put the perfume and ointments on the body but to find that the body is not there at all.

Now their first reaction, and the angel picked up on this, was an absolutely honest reaction. They must have been so scared; they were very, very, afraid. So the first words that the angel speaks to them is "do not be afraid. "Now none of us would question their fear. None of us in the same situation would have had any other kind of reaction than to be afraid because it's a very natural thing, it's a very appropriate response to the situation. All of us would have done the same. But as the story progresses and they take off to fulfill their obligation of proclaiming the resurrection of Jesus Christ, they are met along the way by Jesus himself who greets them and welcomes them. And their response is to throw themselves at his feet and to just hold onto him. And Jesus' words were the same as that of the angel, "do not be afraid. "Now, this is a little different situation in my mind. This isn't the same as seeing an angel, this is not the same as coming into a situation where it is all so miraculous that you don't know what's going on. They are clinging to Jesus' feet. They know they are with the one who loves them, cares for them, the one whom they have worshiped and adored throughout his ministry but yet fear is their response. Why is that? What is it that they are afraid of? What is it that is bringing fear into their hearts, what is it that is causing them to exhibit fear in such a way that Jesus says to them, "do not be afraid. "

I was thinking a lot about that and I was wondering what in the world was going through their minds and I wonder if what Jesus realized was that these poor women had been through the ringer. That, in those three days since Friday, they had thought that their world was absolutely turned up-side down. They thought that nothing was ever going to be the same; they thought that everything they were ever afraid of was coming into fruition. They thought that their hopes were dashed, they thought that their dreams would never be fulfilled - they had put their lives into Jesus' hands, they had put all their hopes and expectations into Jesus' words. And now, they saw him being tortured, they saw him being crucified, they saw him die on the cross and they went to that tomb expecting to anoint the body of one who had devastated their hopes and their dreams. Maybe, just maybe what they were afraid of was the unknown. What they were afraid of was all the changes that they had seen in a short period of time. What they were afraid of was that everything they had dreamed of would never ever come to fruition.

Sound familiar? Does that not sound something like how we're living our lives right now? We had hopes and dreams for Easter Sunday. We had a wonderful Sunrise Service that we had planned. Darren and I were working on some good things for Holy Week and good things for Easter. We thought that this coming Easter was going to be the best Easter ever. That we would pack the church out, that the music would be the best music we've ever heard, maybe, possibly the sermon might be worth listening to (it could happen!). But all of those hopes, all of those expectations, all of those things that we as pastors look forward to and hopefully you as people of this congregation look forward to came to a screeching halt and we find ourselves limited to doing a "second best" kind of thing. Talking to you through a computer, through a screen, a little camera mounted on the top of a computer screen is the means by which we are together. No shaking of hands, no smiling at each other, no greeting each other and asking how each other is doing, no saying to each other, "Happy Easter" and sharing stories of what family is in visiting and so on. We can look at what was lost. We can look ahead and see nothing but fear but that would put us in the same situation as Mary Magdalene and the other Mary on that first Easter morning.

Instead, let us find hope. Let us go forward with hope in our hearts and in our minds. You see, I think that's what Jesus meant when he said, "do not be afraid. "He wanted them to make that choice. They could either remain afraid of what was transpiring, or what was yet to happen or now they could look forward with hope and expectation. You see the scripture tells us that love casts out all fear and what is the Easter message if it is not the fact that absolute love has conquered death and if absolute love can conquer death than it certainly can conquer our fears. You and I have a choice. In light of the resurrection we can live in fear or we can choose the other side and choose to live in hope. For the resurrection of Jesus Christ tells us that hope is sure and well-founded because if God can conquer death, if God can raise Jesus from the grave, if God can roll away that stone and bring Jesus to life, is there anything he can't do? God is able to bring good out of every situation and if we have hope in our hearts and if we live our lives in hope and expectation we will see what it is that God is doing to bring good out of this situation. It's good news on this Easter Sunday. Good news that God's absolute love absolutely conquers everything even the fears in each of our hearts. Absolute love gives us an absolute reason to have hope in each of our hearts and in each of our lives. Let us today, on this Easter Sunday, become the people that are marked by the hope we have in the living of our lives in these trying days and throughout the days that God gives us ahead. Let us look to see what God is doing and let us see how God is using us to share his love his hope in a world that so desperately needs it.

Would you pray with me? O God of grace and God of mercy, we're still amazed these 2,000 years later at the Good News of Jesus Christ. When the women went to find that tomb empty, that empty tomb give us hope. O heavenly Father, fill our hearts with that Good News, fill our lives with that hope that we have that your perfect love can cast out all the fears that are in our hearts this day so that we might live as people of hope sharing your hope in a world that so desperately needs it. We pray all this in Jesus' name and for his sake, Amen.

Walking with Jesus
Luke 24: 13-35

April 26, 2020

The scripture passage that stands before us today is a rather long reading but I would encourage you to follow along with me. It's one of my favorite stories, a post-Easter story. It's after Jesus' resurrection and it's one of those interesting quirky sorts of stories that you read it and your wonder "well I wouldn't have been that way. I would have recognized Jesus as we walked along. "But, I don't know, I don't know if that would be true. I have a hunch that if we were there at the time we would be much like two folks who walked alongside of Jesus on that first day. From the Gospel according to Luke, the 24th chapter beginning with the 13th verse.

"Now the same day two of them were going to a village called Emmaus, about seven miles from Jerusalem. They were talking with each other about everything that had happened. As they talked and discussed these things with each other, Jesus himself came up and walked along with them; but they were kept from recognizing him. He asked them, "What are you discussing together as you walk along?" They stood still, their faces downcast. One of them, named Cleopas asked him, "Are you only a visitor to Jerusalem and do not know the things that have happened there in these days?" "What things?" Jesus asked. "About Jesus of Nazareth," they replied. "He was a prophet, powerful in word and deed before God and all the people. The chief priests and our rulers handed him over to be sentenced to death, and they crucified him; but we had hoped that he was the one who was going to redeem Israel. And what is more, it is the third day since all this took place. In addition, some of our women amazed us. They went to the tomb early this morning but didn't find his body. They came and told us that they had seen a vision of angels, who said he was alive. Then some of our companions went to the tomb and found it just as the women had said, but him they did not see." Jesus said to them, "How foolish you are, and how slow of heart to believe all that the prophets have spoken! Did not the Christ have to

suffer these things and then enter his glory? "And beginning with Moses and all the Prophets, he explained to them what was said in all the Scriptures concerning himself. As they approached the village to which they were going, Jesus acted as if he were going farther. But they urged him strongly, "Stay with us, for it is nearly evening; the day is almost over. "So he went in to stay with them. When he was at the table with them, he took bread, gave thanks, broke it and began to give it to them. Then their eyes were opened and they recognized him, and he disappeared from their sight. Then they asked each other, "were not our hearts burning within us? While he talked with us on the road and opened the scriptures to us? They got up and returned at once to Jerusalem. There they found the 11 and those with them assembled together saying, "It is true! The Lord has risen and appeared to Simon! "Then the two told them what happened on the way and as Jesus recognized by them when he broke the bread. "May the Lord bless this a portion from his holy word.

I'm told that it's about seven miles from Jerusalem to Emmaus. I've never been there so I can't tell you for sure that it is but that's a pretty good walk. I would say a fairly long stretch of road to be able to have a good conversation among the three people walking along that day. We don't know who the two people were. One was Cleopas but we don't know who the other person was. Often times we have scholars who assume that it was two men who were disciples of Jesus but I have a hunch, more than likely, it was a husband and a wife walking along together heading home after a terrible weekend in Jerusalem. They had all the time in the world to talk and to consider and to ponder everything that was happening, all that they had heard, all that they had seen, all that they had hoped for, how their hopes were dashed and their expectations were stolen from them. And they lamented all of this as they walked along. Then Jesus comes along and shares the scriptures bringing things to light with them.

A long walk is a good time to have a good conversation. Last December my family coerced me (in other words, they forced me) into doing the Tacky Light walk (I would not say it was a run - it was not a run for me.)I believe it's a 6 kilometer walk through a neighborhood section of Midlothian and we were doing really good together, all of us were walking together, the extended family and we came to a stop where they had cookies and they had drinks there. Normally, you know me well enough to know that you don't have to offer twice when there's cookies involved. But as we were stopping at that little rest area that they had, I looked to the road ahead of me and I saw that there was a pretty steep series of hills that (at my age and my condition they were steep). To most all of you they weren't that steep but for me they looked awfully steep and I said to Debby, "If I stop now and have to start to go up those hills, I'm not going to make it so I'm just going to keep going. I'll walk slow and all of you can catch up with me. " Well, the rest of the family, being Starzers, took longer with the cookies than would have allowed them catch up with me. So I just kept plodding along putting one foot in front of the other trying to figure out how long this thing was going to take. As I was walking along it was kind of interesting because I got to be a part of all these other groups that were walking along and some of them welcomed me in. Some of them kept a faster pace than me and just walked by but in particular one couple that was a little bit behind me was having an interesting conversation shall we say. I almost thought that I had to turn around and go into my pastoral care mode with the two of them. As we were walking along the organizers marked the progress (of a 6 kilometer walk) in miles and so you would see one mile marker, you would see the two mile marker and three mile marker and so on. As we got to the three mile marker, the couple behind me, I think she had had enough and she turns to her husband and she says, "that's only 3! We go for six and we're only half-way. You told me this was going to be an easy walk and we're not even half-way done yet! " And so I picked up my pace to get ahead of them and stay out of that conversation. I thought it was interesting because a part of me wanted to turn around and say to the woman, "that's three miles not three kilometers. Three miles is a lot more than three kilometers, you're more than half way. You can do this. " I wanted to but I didn't step into it. I kept moving and

I stayed out of that conversation but all I could think about was the fact that this woman was in a miserable mood doing something that she didn't want to do. She got talked into it, obviously, by her husband and she was just going to be miserable If she thought that she was less than half-way done than she was less than half-way done. It didn't matter what the facts of the situation were. She had her mind made up, her eyes were set in a certain place and it was all that she could see. It was a miserable walk, it was too long, she didn't want to do it and that was the end of the discussion. The truth had little or nothing to do with what was happening on that walk.

I think that in some ways what was happening with the two folks and again I'm assuming it was a husband and a wife walking home together, they were lamenting what they saw, lamenting what had happened, just heart-fallen about the situation. Luke tells us that they were crest fallen, that their eyes were downcast. You know how that is, when things are not going the way you want them to go and you're really feeling out of things and you just kind of walk with your head down and you just put one foot in front of the other, well that's how these two people were walking. Their spirits were broken by what happened on that Good Friday. Just three days before, all their hopes and dreams that they had pegged on Jesus were quashed, were stolen from them, were taken away from them and everything they had expected to be the future was now gone from them. Then Jesus comes along and is walking with them and talking with them and you know, I do think that our first instinct is to say "ah I would have recognized him right way, I would have known it was Jesus, I don't know how they could have missed that. "Yet, I think that when you're have that kind of spirit within you, you can't see that which is obvious. You know there's that old saying "the difficult we can handle, the obvious takes a little bit longer" and this would have been one of those cases for that couple. This was a situation where they were handling the difficult but the obvious, that which was right in front of them, took a lot longer for them to see! Their eyes were blinded by what they were feeling, by what they were experiencing, by that sense of loss that they were dealing with in their hearts and lives. As Jesus was talking with them, sharing the scriptures, I'm sure as they later reflected, their hearts were warm within themselves. They were feeling strongly moved by the scriptures that Jesus was sharing with them and they were feeling something special was happening in their hearts as they were listening to Jesus but it wasn't until they got to the house, it wasn't until Jesus sat down with them and began to share a meal with them, a simple meal, that they understood. Obviously they didn't have time to prepare anything fancy or anything special. It was probably just some bread and maybe some fruits, maybe some vegetables that were fresh for that season we don't know, but it was just a simple meal and Jesus took the bread and as he broke it and he was giving it to them, it dawned on them. The whole picture fell together and they began to see that God was doing something good. That God had indeed conquered death. God had indeed brought Jesus back to life; brought Jesus back to be among them. It was in the common and the ordinary, a very simple act of sharing a loaf of bread, one with another that they began to see the work that God was doing.

I think in this season that all of us are going through that it's very easy for us to have those downcast eyes. It would be very easy for us to slip into the mode of thinking only about what we have lost, only thinking about what we are missing, only thinking about the lost opportunities. It's easy to fall into that trap. It's easy to get so caught up in the negative and to look at numbers and statistics to see how many people are afflicted with COVID-19 and how many people have died and to wonder whether the next one is going to be me. It's easy to get caught up in that way of thinking and to find our eyes suddenly downcast and were plodding along just getting through one day at a time, one hour at a time, living our lives as if all hope has been stolen from us. It's an easy trap to fall into. Those two disciples on the road to Emmaus fell into it, many of us can just as easily fall into that trap! But the beauty of what I want to tell you is its simplicity. You see it was in the simple act of a common meal that their eyes were opened and they were able to see the work that God was doing. I think that if we have eyes that are open and if we just look around a little bit, if we just ponder and consider and look at some of the simplest things: small acts of kindness, the beauty of a new day, the ability to have a meal on the table and a roof over our heads, maybe it's in those simplest of things that Jesus will reveal himself to us and we'll see how he is with us and for us, walking alongside us as we go through this time of trail and tribulation with this COVED-19. Pick up your eyes. Don't be downcast. Look and see what God is doing. I'm convinced, absolutely convinced, that God is doing some wonderful things in the life of his church, in the life of his people, in the life of this world through this time of trial and tribulation for us. God is still active and present and we'll see it if we look in the most ordinary places!

Would you pray with me? *Almighty and ever-loving God, we hate to admit it but there are often times, like the couple walking along on the road to Emmaus, we don't see the obvious that is right in front of us. We don't look and see the good things you are doing. We know that you are a God of grace and mercy and love and that you have that extraordinary ability to bring good out of the worst of situations. Help us, O Lord, to look in the simple and the ordinary and the common to see how it is that you are working and moving in this world. Help us to experience your presence with us as you walk alongside us every step along the way this day and every day of our lives. We pray that you would open our eyes. In the name of Jesus, Amen.*

Personal Relationships
John 14: 1-14

May 10, 2020

Our scripture passage for this morning is one that is oftentimes used at funerals. It is a passage that is comforting and hope-filled and I think it is one that is appropriate in any situation and it need not be in the time of losing a loved one but it ought to be one that we can hold onto and cling to in all the situations of our lives. In those situations that frighten us or get us scared, wherever it might be that our emotions are taking us to, to bring us back to the sure and certain foundation that we have in the person and work of Jesus Christ. It's found in the 14th chapter of the Gospel according to John. I invite you to read along with me.

Jesus said, "Do not let your hearts be troubled. Trust in God, trust also in me. In my Father's house are many rooms; if it were not so, I would have told you. I am going there to prepare a place for you. And if I go and prepare a place for you, I will come back and take you to be with me that you may be where I am. You know the way to the place where I am going." Thomas said to him, "Lord, we don't know where you are going, so how can we know the way?" Jesus answered, "I am the way and the truth and the life. No one comes to the Father except through me. If you really knew me, you would know my Father as well. From now on, you do know him and have seen him." Philip said, "Lord, show us the Father and that will be enough for us." Jesus answered: "Don't you know me, Philip, even after I have been among you such a long time? Anyone who has seen me has seen the Father. How can you say, 'Show us the Father?' Don't you believe that I am in the Father, and that the Father is in me? The words I say to you are not just my own. Rather, it is the Father, living in me, who is doing his work. Believe in me, when I say that I am in the Father and the Father is in me; or at least believe on the evidence of the miracles themselves. I tell you the truth, anyone who has faith in me will do what I have been doing. He will do even greater things than these, because I am going to the Father. And I will do whatever you ask in my name, so that the Son may bring glory to the Father.

You may ask me for anything in my name, and I will do it. " May the Lord bless this a portion from his Holy Word.

This is an interesting passage. Out of all the parts of the scripture, I have had some of the most interesting conversations with people about this passage of scripture. It has caused more than one good heart-felt conversation with folks over the years. I remember there was a woman in one of my churches that I served who was adamant to me that the King James was correct and we shouldn't use "houses" that we should use the word "mansions". "In my father's house there are many mansions" she would say. She would talk to me about what she wanted in her mansion and she would just go on and on about how many rooms she wanted in her mansion. She wanted a room for this, she wanted a room for that and a room for another thing and she just had it all clearly visualized in her mind about what the heavenly kingdom was going to be like and it was all about these tangible things. It was all about what her heavenly mansion was going to be like and she was trying to live a good Christian life so that she might get the best mansion possible in the kingdom. She wanted to have the biggest, the best mansion up there and that was what she was striving for in her Christian life. She was absolutely sure that that was what was being promised to her in this passage of scripture from the 14th chapter of John. She was adamant about that and saw all the physical realities of what the heavenly kingdom was going to be like. She was excited and anxious about that day when she would be rewarded with her mansion in the heavenly kingdom.

It didn't matter what I said, how I said it, how I explained it or how I tried to talk her through this: that it wasn't the physical thing that Jesus was talking about. If you listen carefully in this passage of scripture Jesus is talking about relationship. It says, "I am going to prepare a place for you so I will come again and bring you to be with me. How do we know the way? Well, I am the way, I am the truth I am that life for you. It's all about the relationship. What is the kingdom of heaven look like? We don't know. We don't know what it's going to look like. But we're going to know what it entails. What makes it heaven? It's simply the presence of Jesus Christ.

You know, it's John, the writer of this gospel that included this dialogue between Jesus and his disciples but he also was the one who said that God is love. Jesus is trying to show to us that he is the second person of the trinity. I think this is one of the passages of scripture that brings out the nature of the trinity most clearly in my mind, in my thinking. And Jesus is trying to say that if you have seen me, Jesus, then you have seen the Father. There is that unity, that integrity between the Father and the Son and if you want to know what heaven is going to be like, it's going to be being in the presence of absolute love. And if you're in the presence of absolute love, if you are in that situation where you are so filled and so surrounded by love, do you think you're going to care how big your house is? Do you think you're going to care about how many rooms your mansion might have? Do you think you're going to care whether the streets are paved with gold or are dirt or brick or stone? I don't think it's going to make a bit of difference because the nature of heaven in and of itself is the very presence of Jesus Christ. Absolute love: for God is love and God has revealed that love to us through his son Jesus Christ.

And if that is indeed the fact then I really and truly believe that Jesus is trying to get across to us then I think it has a profound impact upon how we live our lives in the here and now. Therefore, if Jesus is the way then we need to follow that way. If being with Jesus in that element of absolute love is what the heavenly kingdom is all about, then isn't it just possible that we get to experience a bit of the heavenly kingdom in the here and now? Isn't it quite possible that whenever we find ourselves drawing closer to our Lord and Savior Jesus Christ that we are in those moments experiencing his love? Experiencing love that God has for us knows no beginning and knows no end. Isn't it in those moments that we get a glimpse, maybe a little bit of an experience of what the heavenly kingdom is all about? Isn't it in those moments that we experience a little bit of what absolute love is? If we have those experiences does it not change how we look at the things around us? The beauty of this world is a little bit more beautiful. Things we might have thought one time of absolute importance seem to be meaningless. Isn't it also true that maybe some of the things that you and I tend to worry about aren't worth worrying about at all?

If we experience the presence of Jesus Christ in our hearts and in our lives, we're going to see a little bit more clearly what's important and what's not so important. I think that this situation with the COVID-19 virus is giving us an opportunity to look at our lives a little bit more clearly, to recognize what is important and what is not important, to recognize how important love is for each of us in our lives and if we have that love within our lives then everything else is secondary. All of a sudden making an extra few dollars takes a secondary place to being a better father, brother, sister, mother, friend. All those things start to grow in importance over against how many dollars are in our savings account or how big our house might be. You see, Jesus was trying to encourage his disciples and in fact encourage you and me to see that the kingdom of heaven is as near as our hearts. Now, I'm not saying there won't be that day when we fully experience it, that is something that we all have in our future for us but what I am saying is don't wait. Allow that love to be a part of your life here and now. To allow Jesus' love to become that which helps you to focus your life to see what's important and what's not so important. Would you pray with me?

Our heavenly Father we do give you thanks for your Son Jesus Christ who lived among us and showed us the depth, the breath and the height of your love toward each and every one of us. We give you thanks O Lord for that gift to us, a glimpse of your love, a glimpse of experiencing the heavenly kingdom in our hearts and in our lives in the here and now and the here and after. We give you thanks for the name of Jesus Christ who alone is our Lord and Savior. Amen.

Knowing God by Name
Acts 17: 22-31

May 17, 2020

Our scripture lesson for this morning is a familiar one to many of us I'm sure. It's a wonderful story out of the Book of Acts in the 17th chapter of the Acts of the Apostles. It's a story of Paul's travels that took him into the Greek country and here he finds himself in Athens and let's pick up on the story in the 17 chapter of the Acts of the Apostles in the 22nd verse:

"Paul stood in front of the Aeropagus and said: "Anthenians! I see how extremely religious you are in every way. For as I went through the city and looked carefully at the objects of your worship, I found among them an altar with the inscription: TO AN UNKNOWN GOD. What therefore you worship as unknown, this I proclaim to you. The God who made the world and everything in it, he who is Lord of heaven and earth does not live in shines made by human hands nor is he served by human hands as though he needed anything since he himself gives to all mortals life and breath and all things. From one ancestor he made all nations to inhabit the whole earth. And he allotted the times of their existence and the boundaries of the places where they would live so that they would search for God and perhaps grope for him and find him though indeed He is not far from each one of us. For in him we live and move and have our being and even as some of your own poets have said for we too are his offspring. Since we are God's offspring we ought not to think that the deity is like gold or silver or stone in an image formed by the art and the imagination of mortals. While God has overlooked the times of human ignorance, now he commands all people everywhere to repent. Because he has fixed a day on which he will have the world judged in righteousness by a man whom he has appointed and of this he has given assurance to all by raising him from the dead. 'May the Lord bless this a portion from his holy word.

When I was in seminary one of the most challenging courses that I ever took was a course on 2nd Corinthians taught by Dr. Cullen I K

Story a professor of Greek New Testament. In this particular course the requirements were very demanding, at least in my mind they were very demanding. We had to translate the entire book of 2nd Corinthians from Greek into English and alongside of that while we were doing that (that was a struggle in itself that took a great deal of time and energy and a lot of hard work to do) we were required to read two books of <u>Brothers Karamazov</u> and <u>Crime and Punishment</u>. Neither of which are easy books to read, neither of which are small books to read, both of them have hundreds and hundreds and hundreds of pages in them. As I was reading the first one, Brothers Karamazov, I was just struggling. I could not figure it out, I was not getting the lot, I could not figure out who all of the characters were in the book - it wasn't making any sense to me in any way, shape or form. And so, as I'm struggling to get through this and I'm working my way through this, it was required and I had to do it; it wasn't something that I could put off to the side and say well I'll just do this some other time in my life, maybe I'll get more out of it then. It was a required part of the course to read these books and interact them with the text of 2nd Corinthians. But it finally dawned on me after about 300 and so pages, that in <u>Brothers Karamazov</u>, there was a clue that I had missed. I had missed the fact or I didn't understand the fact that in the Russian culture in which Dostoevsky was writing, people had three different names. They had a very formal name, a name that you would use if the relationship was extremely formal if you were greeting a person of superior office than yours, you would use the formal name. And then there was (what I would call) the semi-formal name and that would be one that would be used among friends and those you work with side-by-side and so on, the semi-formal name and then they had a third name for those who were closest to the person and that name would be what we might call a nickname. It was used within family among brothers and sisters, parent and child and the closest of relations would use that informal name. So it took me a long time to figure out that the same person could be referred to with three different names. I would say that there were three different people but there's actually just one person who was known by a variety of names. And that's important to learn if you're going to read something like Dostoevsky because knowing the name helps you understand the person. And in that case knowing the name also helped you to understand the relationships that that person held, where they were and how they related to that other person as equals, or as superiors or as close family. The use of the name was so helpful in understanding what was happening.

And I think Paul sensed that in his arrival in Athens that the Athenians were indeed a very religious people and he found so in the situation where they had gathered from all sorts of areas, all sorts of places in order to have good discussions. This Aeropagus was a place where people would gather to exchange ideas and thoughts and philosophies, talk about current events, talk about big picture things or whatever it was that was on their minds and it was in a surrounding that lent itself to their current religious situation. It was surrounded by these different altars and so on that were described to the different gods of the Greek culture of the time and each one of them had their own idol from stone or fine metals like gold or silver what have you. They were all carved and very beautiful and each one of them had a name, each one of them had a purpose but Paul stumbled across one that simply had this inscription: TO AN UNKNOWN GOD. Paul wanted them to see that this god who they know as unknown is highly knowable. And not only highly knowable but Paul could introduce this god to them by name through the person and work of Jesus Christ.

You see God reveals himself through the person and work of Jesus Christ, reveals the personality of God, the very nature of who God is through who Jesus Christ is, shows to us who God truly is and who we are more importantly in relationship to that one true God. Paul didn't want them to live in ignorance, he did not want them to have an unknown god, he wanted them to know the one true living God. The one in whom we have our life our breath, we have our every movement. Our life is centered in this one true God and he wanted them to know who this God is and how this God wanted to be in relationship with them because he goes on to talk about how we are God's offspring. Introducing the thought to those people serving an unknown god that this unknown god to them was not just a god but was their heavenly Father who wanted to love them and care for them, to be with them and for them.

Now we live in a time where we look at something like this and we think, that's just not who we are. We would never, any of us, have a stone carved or wooden carving or some other idol placed on the mantels in our homes to bow down and worship and to pray to that idol for our needs or wants, whatever it was that we had our heart's desire set for. That's not our style, that's not a way that we do things, that's not the way that we live our lives. We're not that kind of people. It's not a part of our heritage or our culture, it's not a part of our traditions. We don't set up little idols in the corner and bow down and worship them. But, on the other hand, are there not idols in our lives where we place our trust and our hope? Isn't it quite possible that in each of our lives we find those places that we put our hope and we seek our comfort that may or may not be our wisest choice.

In this difficult time that we find ourselves living, it's easy for us to get caught up in the news cycle that comes out and maybe we place too much trust in this particular news service or this particular news anchor or particular commentator. Maybe we put all of our trust in a particular doctor that we heard on T. V. or maybe we put all of our trust in a particular politician in whom we think is going to be the one who cares for us and takes care of us. Or maybe we put all trust in having a few extra dollars put away in the bank or I don't know where it is but we have this tendency to find these false idols. These places that we put our hope and our trust, that are not sure, that are not certain and oftentimes fail us. Who among us hasn't been disappointed by some politician and the word that they offered being so far away from the word that they delivered? Or who of us hasn't been disappointed to find out that something we were told to be true turns out not to be true? I'm so glad that Marcy read for us this morning a wonderful quote from the Heidelberg catechism as to where our one true hope and comfort is found and it's found in the Lord our Savior whether in life or in death, we belong to God. There is the one true God who we know by name, who we call our Father in heaven, who we know is Jesus living among us and with us for us; not some unknown God. The one who has proved himself to us time and time and time again, one where we place all of our hope, all of our trust, one in whom we can find our ultimate comfort, can find the peace that we are looking for in these days of trial and struggle. We are blessed because God has revealed himself to us so that we might know him, love him, cherish him, enjoy him and find all the comfort that we desire in that love and in that grace that he offers to us.

Would you pray with me? Our heavenly Father we do give you thanks for your son Jesus Christ in whom we find our one true life, that life is found in your love. Help us O Lord not to chase after false idols, to seek our comfort elsewhere, to seek our hope elsewhere but to always seek our comfort and hope in your grace and in your love. We pray this all in Jesus' name and for his sake. Amen.

Hurry Up and Wait
Acts 1: 6-14

May 24, 2020

Believe it or not this is the seventh Sunday of Easter, the last Sunday of Eastertide and next Sunday upon our soft reopening, we will be into the season of Pentecost so we're making a transition here. On this last Sunday of the season of Easter, we take a look at the Acts of the Apostles, in the first chapter, verses 6-14 there. Not altogether unfamiliar to many, but one that ought to be familiar to all of us as we deal with the days we're living in. So let's take a look at Acts 1, verses 6-14:

"In my former book, Theophilus, I wrote about all that Jesus began to do and to teach until the day he was taken up to heaven, after giving instructions through the Holy Spirit to the apostles he had chosen. After his suffering, he showed himself to these men and gave many convincing proofs that he was alive. He appeared to them over a period of forty days and spoke about the kingdom of God. On one occasion, while he was eating with them, he gave them this command: "Do not leave Jerusalem, but wait for the gift my Father promised which you have heard me speak about. For John baptized with water, but in a few days you will be baptized with the Holy Spirit. "

So when they met together, they asked him, "Lord, are you at this time going to restore the kingdom of Israel?

He said to them: "It is not for you to know the times or dates the Father has set by his own authority. But you will receive power when the Holy Spirit comes on you; and you will be my witnesses in Jerusalem, and in all Judea and Samaria and to the ends of the earth. "

After he said this, he was taken up before their very eyes, and a cloud hid him from their sight.

They were looking intently up into the sky as he was going, when suddenly two men dressed in white stood beside them. "Men of Galilee," they said, "why do you stand here looking into the sky? This same Jesus, who has been taken from you into heaven, will come back in the same way you have seen him go into heaven."

Then they returned to Jerusalem from the hill called the Mount of Olives, a Sabbath day's walk from the city. When they arrived, they went upstairs to the room where they were staying. Those present were Peter, John, James and Andrew; Philip and Thomas, Bartholomew and Matthew; James son of Alphaeus and Simon the Zealot, and Judas son of James. They all joined together constantly in prayer, along with the women and Mary the mother of Jesus, and with his brothers. 'May the Lord bless this a portion from his Holy Word.

Boy if there ever there seemed to be an appropriate text to be thinking about during this time, this very well may be the text that we all need to hear; these words that were spoken and dialogue between Jesus and his disciples. The disciples were, to say the least, were an anxious bunch. They wanted to know everything, they wanted plan everything, they wanted to get the whole picture. They wanted to have everything all squared away for them and as Jesus is meeting with them for what would be one last time before his ascension, they asked him the question, "Is this the time? Is this the time when you are going to restore the kingdom of Israel? Is this the time when everything is going to come together? Is this the time when everything that's wrong is going to be made right? Is this the time when we are going to be able to enjoy the fruits of your labor?"They were anxious to know "what's the schedule here? How much longer are we going to have to put up with this hiding out in an upper room? How much longer are we going to have to be scared and worried and confused? How much longer are we going to have to be dealing with the unknown? How much longer are we going to have to go on like this? "Does that sound like anybody you might know? Does that sound like some of the questions that you and I might have in our hearts right now? Does it sound like some of the prayers that we have lifted? Lord is this the time when you're going to end the COVID-19? O Lord is this the time when we're going to be able to get back to normal? O Lord is this the time when all this is going to come to an end? We want to know the dates and the times so we pray and we hope and we long for and we look for the answers to those questions because we want to get back to the way things were.

The disciples were anxious to restore the kingdom of Israel, to get back to glory days of what it meant to be a Jewish believer in the one true God. They wanted to get back to what used to be and what would yet be again someday. We are anxious, we are fearful, we are confused, we are a lot of different emotions and we want to know when this is all going to end. We want to know when this is all going to come to conclusion as if something is going to happen then BOOM it's as if it never happened. We want to know if it's tomorrow, the next day, another week or another two weeks. Just give us the dates Lord. Tell us the date. We just want to be able to plan to have a goal in mind so we can get back to enjoying our lives the way that we used to enjoy them so much.

Understandably, normal. It's the way we all are. I'm no different than any of you. I want things to be back to normal. I want to be standing in front of you, I want to be shaking your hand, I want to be looking you in the eye, I want to be enjoying your company, I want to be back to normal. As much as, maybe even more so than many others. That's my hope, my dream. I would love to know if it's one more month, two more months? How long is it going to be? Is this the time, is this the discovery, is this the cure, is this the treatment, is this the vaccine? I want to know. So we find ourselves being no different than those disciples there on the Mount of Olives with Jesus that day asking that question. Is this the time? And Jesus' answer probably was not very satisfying to the disciples, probably didn't bring them a lot of comfort. He says, "Well, you know what? You don't know. It's not for you to know. It's not under your purview of things to be concerned about. God has everything in his own timing. The Father has got things under control. Why are you worried about dates and times?"

Now there's another element to this. It's not just the fact that Jesus said, "It's not for you to know. The Father has got everything under control. Everything is going to be okay. God's got this in hand and we need to rely on that. "I'm not diminishing the answer that Jesus gave. I'm not saying that wasn't something we need to hear because we do need to hear that. We do need to hear that God is in control and God has everything in hand and that God will take care of us, whether we live or we die, we belong to the Lord. That's the Gospel truth. That's the way that we live our lives. What I am saying is that Jesus told them a little bit more as well. He instructed them what to do. You know I am very anxious about getting the church back to normal. I am anxious about gathering everybody in, reestablishing our worship services, getting the choir back in the choir loft, the people back in the pews, the Praise Band up on the podium and I am just anxious to have all of that taking place. I want the church to be back to normal, I want the church to get back to what it should do, can do and ought to do. But, Jesus is also very straight here with his disciples. While you are all worrying about the times and the dates, here's what you're going to do. You're going to go back to Jerusalem and you're going to be my witnesses there, you're going to be my witnesses in an ever expanding ministry that you're going to have. In other words, Jesus was telling his disciples don't worry about being the kingdom of Israel, be worried about doing the work that you're called to do.

I think that that's been a tough lesson but a good lesson for us in the midst of all this pandemic, that we are still the church with the work of the church to do in spite of the pandemic. The work of the church has not stopped for one minute. Yes, we can't be together, yes we can't have Bible study in the church and we can't do a lot of different things. There are a lot of things we can't do but we can't get hung up on what can't do. What we need to see is what God is calling us to do and there have been so many areas of ministry that have grown during this pandemic, different ways of serving others and to our community and to even those outside of our community. We have been there with people and for people helping them out. I have heard so many wonderful stories about people who have been calling on others, making phone calls, checking up on people and just making sure they're okay and that's heartwarming. That's the church being the church. And I know that it takes time and I know that it takes energy because we're all fenced in and we want to be with people so oftentimes in my experience a simple call that I think is going to take five or ten minutes ends up taking an hour or so because the conversations are so good and we don't want the good conversations to draw to a conclusion.

You see Jesus didn't want us to worry about when things were going to happen, didn't want us to think that we had to plan and control everything. He just wants us to do the work of the church. He just wants us to be his people in this world sharing his love, sharing his grace, sharing his mercy. If ever there was a time when we needed to do that, if ever there was a time that love needs to be our watch word and our by word, now is that time. When people are afraid, it is we the church that can offer them peace. When people are worried, it is we the church who can assuage those concerns. When people are feeling lonely and isolated, it is we the church who can remind them that we are all together as brothers and sisters, as God's sons and daughters. You see the disciples missed that. The disciples missed that point all together, there were so anxious to enjoy the rewards of all they had gone through, they had spent forty days with the resurrected Jesus and after that period of three days of abject discouragement, they were now feeling hope again and they wanted to get on with it and they wanted to see the kingdom come in all of its glory. We know that James and John were anxious to see which one got to sit on Jesus' left and which one got to sit at Jesus' right hand. They had this image in mind of the glory and the greatness. What Jesus had in mind was love, compassion, service, making his grace, his mercy, his love, his peace known to a world that so desperately needs to hear it.

So as we're anxious, and I'm anxious to get back to whatever normal might mean to us, let's remember to keep doing the work that Jesus Christ has called us to do - to be his people, to share his love, to do his work within our world.

Would you pray with me? O loving heavenly father, we thank you that ultimately you are in control. We sometimes lose sight of that fact. We sometimes think that this world depends upon us, the skill of our planning, the skill of our execution but what the world really needs is ourselves, our love, our compassion that we have experienced through you in order that we might share it with others. Help us O Lord to be your people, to do your work, to follow your will no matter what the circumstances of our life may be, no matter where we may be, we know that there is work for us to do, to share your love in this world. We pray this in Jesus' name and for his sake, Amen.

Sheltering in Place
Acts 2: 1-13

May 31, 2020

Today is Pentecost Sunday and there is a lot of good irony in this fact that it is Pentecost Sunday. Pentecost being what we traditionally celebrate as the birth of the Christian church, that it was on Pentecost that the church was empowered with the Holy Spirit and enabled to become what it is called to be. And so there is that certain irony that this is the first Sunday that we are in some semblance or form re-birthing the church here at Fairfield as a gathering body, limited though it may be and appropriately so because we don't want anybody to here and be uncomfortable or at risk of anything so. We look at the second chapter of Acts in the first 13 verses:

"When the day of Pentecost came, they were all together in one place. Suddenly a sound like the blowing of a violent wind came from heaven and filled the whole house where they were sitting. They saw what seemed to be tongues of fire that separated and came to rest on each of them. All of them were filled with the Holy Spirit and began to speak in other tongues as the Spirit enabled them.

Now there were staying in Jerusalem God-fearing Jews from every nation under heaven. When they heard this sound, a crowd came together in bewilderment, because each one heard them speaking in his own language. Utterly amazed, they asked: "Are not all these men who are speaking Galileans? Then how is it that each of us hears them in his own native language? Parthians, Medes and Elamites; residents of Mesopotamia, Judea and Cappadocia, Pontus and Asia, Phrygia and Pamphylia, Egypt and the parts of Libya near Cyrene; visitors from Rome; Cretans and Arabs - we hear them declaring the wonders of God in our own tongues! "Amazed and perplexed, they asked one another, "What does this mean?"

Some, however, made fun of them and said, "They have had too much wine. "May the Lord bless this a portion from his holy word.

You know there is a striking similarity I would say between the first Pentecost and today. Not so much in what you might think of, you don't see any tongues of flames sitting above our heads and we don't have anybody speaking in a foreign language, do we? You're all good with English? But the similarity is this - did you notice where this day started? First day of Pentecost, Pentecost. It started when they were all huddled together in their house. The word quarantine means 40 days. It is an old word that comes from what many ports did if a ship came in from a distant land, they had to be quarantined, they had to spend 40 days before they would be allowed off the ship and into the country that was receiving them. But for the disciples of Jesus they had done the quarantine plus ten. They had just spent 50 days huddled together, 50 days living in fear, wondering what might happen next. They spent 50 days being confused and uncertain about what the future was going to hold. Oh they knew certain things, they knew, or at least they wanted to know, they wanted to believe that Jesus was alive, that he was raised from the grave. They wanted to believe that, they struggled to believe that, you hear time and time again that they saw Jesus in his resurrection state, they struggled to believe. But they had that, at least that bit of knowledge that death had been conquered and that Jesus was alive but they weren't sure what it meant. They weren't sure what it was going to mean for them, how it was going to impact their lives, what was going to be different, what was tomorrow going to look like. What would this new normal be for them? They didn't know. They had probably some good conversations among themselves in that house where they were hold up, in that house where they were self-quarantined, they probably had some great conversations about what might be happenings and they probably ranged everywhere from abject fear to absolute hope and probably everything in-between. Because when you're not certain that's how your mind works. Your mind goes from one to the other and back again with a few stops along the way as it's bouncing back and forth.

It seems to me there is a good similarity between what we have been living and what those early disciples were going through in their lives and then a curve ball is thrown at them. I don't think any of them were sitting there counting the days going "this is 50 days, Pentecost, that's an old Jewish celebration, 50 days after the Passover is a celebration. . . " I don't think anyone was probably counting that, I don't think any of them expected what transpired. Not that they shouldn't have expected it, let's be honest about that. If they had been listening to what Jesus was teaching them, they would have known what was coming because Jesus promised them the Comforter, the Holy Spirit, the Holy One who would be with them to help them, give them the words to speak and so on. If they had been listening, if they had kind of fathomed what that would mean, they would have had some expectation of what happened on that first Pentecost Sunday. But it appears that they didn't. They were probably as surprised as any of us would have been in the same situation, surprised by the presence of the Holy Spirit coming and resting upon them and giving them not just the right words to speak because we all hope for that, we all pray for that. You know when going into a difficult situation or we're meeting with somebody or visiting somebody who is ill or lost a loved one or lost a job and we pray Lord give me the right words to speak. Well, not only did the Holy Spirit give them the right words to speak but he gave them the right languages in which to speak it - multiple languages. It's hard to picture what that might have looked like, but it seems as if each of the disciples were given the ability to communicate to somebody who was gathered there from all those different lands. He gave them the ability to speak in the native tongue. Form all those visitors, from all those strange places that probably none of those disciples had ever been to and most of them probably hadn't ever heard of them. God gave them what they needed when they needed it to do what needed to be done.

I think there's a lesson there for us is there not? Sure we're aware of the Holy Spirit and aware of the work of the Holy Spirit and comfortable with the thought of the Holy Spirit guiding and directing us and dwelling within us giving us comfort and encouragement when we need it. We're okay with that, we're comfortable with that but the lesson here is a little bit more than just "O Holy Spirit what have you done for me lately? "It's the fact the disciples were given what they needed, when they needed it to do what they needed to do. You see it wasn't about what do I get out of this? It wasn't about "Lord give me the strength to do this or that or the other thing because I really want to do this that or the other thing. "It's about looking for God to give us the strength, the ability, the right words, to be in the right place at the right time to spread his word of love. And I don't know what that looks like. I mean I wish I could tell you that here's what you should do, here's what you should do, here's what you should do, here's what you should do. What it is, is having an open heart to look beyond ourselves.

It is so easy, it is so absolutely easy in a time like this to turn in and be self-centered, to mumble, to grumble and complain. I hate these silly masks. I will grumble and complain about wearing this. Trust me. Ask Debby if you don't believe me. I don't like a lot of things that this COVID-19 has brought upon us. I don't like the fact that we can't pack out this room with everybody that we know and love. I don't like the fact that we have somebody in the hospital right now, a member of this church for many, many years, and I can't stop in to see him. I don't like that. There are a lot of things I don't like about this COVID-19 and trust me I could spend a lot of time telling you all the things that I am complaining about. I'll bet you and I could get some good conversations going if I asked you, "How are you doing with all of this?" It is easy to become self-centered, to think about what we've lost, what we don't have, what we miss, what we wish but that's not what we're called to do. That's not who we're called to be. We need to have open hearts to see what it is God is calling us to do. To serve in a time such as this and it may very well be that the presence of the Holy Spirit is already moving in your hearts and in your lives and you are already doing what you're called to do because the Spirit is already tugging at your hearts pushing you in the right direction, helping you to have the right words, to speak the right things at the right times. But you have to have that open heart, that willingness to let the Spirit move you and guide you and direct you. We talk about there being a "new normal," I'm not sure what that phrase even means because there is no such thing as the "old normal" because God's work is fresh and new every day. And

I really believe in my heart that God is able to turn even the worst of situations into something good but we have to participate in that work. I believe that God is doing a new thing in his church. I'm not sure what that is yet, I'm not sure how it's going to look, but I think that the Christian church and hopefully Fairfield Church will come through this stronger with a greater sense of our purpose in this community and in our world to do God's work and to do God's mission, to be a light in a darkened world. I don't think the disciples on that Pentecost really knew what was going to come along. If they saw the Christian church in the four corners of the world as it is today, they would just be amazed that that gift of the Holy Spirit on that day started all of that. We don't know how this is all going to work out and how God is going to use us but we know that he will. If our hearts are open and we desire to be his people, doing his work in this world today.

Would you pray with me? Almighty and ever loving God, we give you thanks for the gift of your Holy Spirit who dwells within us, tugging at our hearts, pushing us in the right direction. Help us O Lord to be open to the work of the Holy Spirit in each of our lives so that we might indeed speak your word of love through our words, through our actions, through our presence, through the compassion that you give to each of us. We pray this in Jesus' name and for his sake, Amen.

Holy Trinity with Us
Matthew 28: 16-20

June 6, 2020

Today is Trinity Sunday in the Christian calendar. I love the fact that as they were setting up the Christian calendar so many, many, years ago that they took the most difficult concept in Christian theology and gave it one Sunday. So one Sunday out of the year it becomes incumbent upon the preacher to try and explain the meaning of the Trinity. So how does one explain the meaning of the Trinity? There have been all sorts of analogies given over the years, all sorts of different ways to look at understanding the Trinity; some of them make more sense, some of them make less sense, some of them are analogies such as water in three different forms is still water whether it's steam, whether it's ice, or whether it's water, it's still three different things in one thing in actuality. That may be one of the closest to come to an understanding but that doesn't explain the nature of relationship because the Trinity is about relationship. The Trinity is by its nature relational and so others have tried the analogy of a single person can be a father, a son, an uncle but still the same person, just the different relationships with others is the definition of who that person is in those situations. Again, not a bad analogy, but not a full complete analogy. So let me try this for all of us today. Let me try to help our understanding of the Trinity from just a slightly different perspective. I don't know if academically it will satisfy anybody's minds as to comprehend the Trinity but maybe in a relational sense it might give us a little better understanding of what it means to be people who serve a triune God, the Father, Son and Holy Ghost.

So let's take a look at a very familiar passage, one that may be or may be not is thought of when it comes to understanding the Trinity. It's at the tail end of the Gospel according to Matthew in the 28th chapter there picking up in the 16th verse:

"Then the eleven disciples went to Galilee, to the mountain where Jesus had told them to go. When they saw him, they worshiped him; but some doubted. Then Jesus came to them and said, "All authority in heaven and on earth has been given to me. Therefore go and make disciples of all nations, baptizing them in the name of the Father and of the Son and of the Holy Spirit, and teaching them to obey everything I have commanded you. And surely I am with you always, to the very end of the age. 'May the Lord bless this a portion from his holy word.

The Trinity, Father, Son, Holy Spirit or Holy Ghost whichever your preference might be is, by its very nature, relational. That each part of the Trinity, each person of the Trinity is in relationship with the other persons of the Trinity in a unity, in a cohesion, in a binding together that is mutually exclusive of anything of any one person of the trinity doing anything that can be contradictory to any other person of the Trinity. In other words, the Holy Spirit will never lead you to do something that is contrary to what Jesus taught us to do. And Jesus would never have led us in a way that God our Father didn't want us to go. There is that consistency within the Trinity, that perfect unity, that perfect consistency among the three persons of the Trinity. And it's all about what you're doing because the Trinity is also all about relationships with each one of us. God created us. God the Father, creator of all, Jesus Christ the Son came to redeem us, to teach us, to restore us back to whom we were called to be in the first place and the Holy Spirit dwells within us and among us to guide us and direct us to be His equal in this time and in this place. It's all about relationships. It's all about being together.

Within the creation account in Genesis, God looks and says, "Let us make them in our image. "God speaks of himself in that Trinitarian formula in the very creation and expresses his desire to create beings that are like as God is. Now that doesn't mean that he created little gods but what it means is that he created us to be in relationship with him and be in relationship with each other. That's central to the person of who God is: love. Love for one another, love for God,

God's love for us that we have seen in Jesus Christ and experienced through the Holy Spirit. And so we are all created in the very image of God to be in relationship one with another but we live in a fallen world. We live in a world where we have taken what God has created and we've made a mess of it. I hate to be that blunt but the facts are what the facts are. Because God created us to live one with another, to see each other as brothers and sisters in God's great creation, to see each other as a creation of God and when we start to break people down into categories, whatever groups it might be we cease to love one another. I was talking with a good friend last night and he is so worried that we are going to end up being a nation where everybody has a stamp on his forehead, whether a "D" or an "R" and that the "D's" can't talk to the "Rs" and the "Rs" can't talk to the "D's". We have this terrible habit as human beings of dividing, of isolating, of setting others to the side and elevating ourselves by seeking to diminish others. That does such a disservice to the God who created us, to the God who redeemed us, to the God who sustains us because it is a denial of our relationships. It is a denial of our relationship with God. God doesn't see republican or democrat, God doesn't see white or black or Asian, or any other different category that we put people in. God sees each of us as his creation, as his sons and his daughters. God has no favorite children. There is that unity in God's love, the unity that we see in the Trinity. There is that consistency in God's love, that there is nobody, no one, no where, no how who is outside of the grasp of God's love. In a moment that we in any way, shape or form exclude anyone from God's love, we are going contrary to who God is. The Trinity stands before us as that great sign of what it means to be in relationship in a consistent and loving way. Three persons, each uniquely suited for the purpose of loving us, each human being is perfectly suited to be loved by God and to be loved by each of us.

We live in a difficult time, there's no sugar coating that. These are challenging days that we find ourselves in. There is much anger, there is much hatred, there are a lot of loud voices - no shortage of loud voices-but what we need more of and where the Christian church needs to be is at the effort to exhibit and example of how we treat one another in love. That ability to show respect to somebody, even if they are 180 degrees opposed to everything that you believe in. To love and respect, to listen to them and hopefully they will listen to you. But we need to be the practitioners of love. We need to be the ones who show that there is a better way, a more excellent way as the Apostle Paul says, the way of love - because love never fails. We're human beings and we fall short all the time but love never fails. The God of us all, the Lord and Father of us all, his Son Jesus Christ, the ever present Holy Spirit are with us, to guide and direct us to learn how to model love, kindness, grace and mercy so that there might be a greater love in our world. It's time for us not to take sides; it's time for us to practice love and grace. It's time for us to show the world that there is that more excellent way. Would you pray with me?

Almighty and ever loving God, you are our ever present help in times of trouble. So we know that you are here. We know that you are with us. We know that you are with our community, you are with our country, you are with our world. Help us to tap into that love. Help us to be your bearers of grace and good news, to share that love in such a way that more people come to you, indeed, that we might make more disciples, that we might baptize more people into your love. Give us the right words, give us the ability to listen, give us the compassion to care. We pray all this in Jesus' name and for his sake, Amen.

Never Abandoned
Genesis 21: 8-21

June 21, 2020

Now, over the years, I have done any number of faux pas as a pastor. I remember early on in my ministry in Wyalusing on Mother's Day I had an ill-chosen hymn. On that particular Mother's Day I chose that we should sing the hymn "Come, Labor On. "That did not go over well. I did have a funeral that I was asked to do one time and I got there and realized I could not remember the name of the deceased. Another faux pas under my belt. Now as you hear this passage of scripture today that is found in the book of Genesis in the 21st chapter, your first thought might be I've added another faux pas to my list because as you hear this text you are going to think, Steve, did you really choose this one for Father's Day? So let's take a look at this and see whether or not I have goofed again. In the 21st chapter of the Book of Genesis, verses 8-21 we have this very interesting story:

"The child grew and was weaned, and on the day Isaac was weaned Abraham held a great feast. But Sarah saw that the son whom Hagar the Egyptian had borne to Abraham was mocking, and she said to Abraham, "Get rid of that slave woman and her son, for that slave woman's son will never share in the inheritance with my son Isaac. The matter distressed Abraham greatly because it concerned his son. But God said to him, "Do not be so distressed about the boy and your maidservant. Listen to whatever Sarah tells you, because it is through Isaac that your offspring will be reckoned. I will make the son of the maidservant into a nation also, because he is your offspring. "Early the next morning Abraham took some food and a skin of water and gave them to Hagar. He set them on her shoulders and then sent her off with the boy. She went on her way and wandered in the desert of Beersheba. When the water in the skin was gone, she put the boy under one of the bushes. Then she went off and sat down nearby, about a bowshot away, for she thought, "I cannot watch the boy die. "And as she sat there nearby, she began to sob. God heard the boy crying and

the angel of God called to Hagar from heaven and said to her, "What is the matter, Hagar? Do not be afraid; God has heard the boy crying as he lies there. Lift the boy up and take him by the hand, for I will make him into a great nation. "Then God opened her eyes and she saw a well of water. So she went and filled the skin with water and gave the boy a drink. God was with the boy as he grew up. He lived in the desert and became an archer. While he was living in the Desert of Paran, his mother got a wife for him from Egypt. 'May the Lord bless this a portion from His Holy Word.

You know I've talked in the past about certain passages of scripture that are "favorites" of ours - counted cross stitch passages that I talk about. Ones that you would want to have on the wall of your living room to be a good reminder and something to cling to and find hope and peace in. This is not one of those passages. This is definitely not a counted cross stitch passage for us. This is more of a "boy this one troubles me" passage. The story of Abraham and Sarah, Hagar, Ishmael, Isaac, one messed up situation. I mean it was Sarah's idea. Sarah was the one who said to Abraham, "I'm never going to be able to give you children. Why don't you take my maid servant here and have a child with her and that will carry on your lineage. You can have a son through her and that will take care of everything. I'm never going to be able to give you the child you so desperately want. The child that God had promised to you. "It was Sarah's idea in the first place. But it didn't work out so well.

God's promise to Abraham and Sarah came to fulfillment and Isaac was born, the longed for son. The son of their senior years came to them and now the family dynamics were all changed. Now Sarah had the job of protecting her son from the older son and she was not going to have any competition against her son. So she said to Abraham, "I don't care what you do, I don't care what happens to them. I want them out of here. I don't want to have that interloper anywhere near you. You have Isaac now, you have no need for Ishmael. "Now this is also one of those awkward passages because God comes on to the scene and takes Sarah's side. Not exactly what we would have guessed, not exactly what we would have expected and there are some thoughts that this is, if we went back to the original Hebrew that what God said to Abraham was, "Happy wife, happy life" but we don't know for sure that that's exactly what God might have said them. But it's an awkward situation. God makes a promise in that situation. God said "I'll take care of him, don't you worry about him. "And so Hagar and her son Ishmael are sent off with some provisions, probably what they thought would be enough provisions to get them to some place where they could settle in and start to make a good life for themselves. Maybe they could get back to Egypt among the Egyptian people to settle down and have a good life there. But as it worked out those provisions didn't make it very long. It wasn't nearly enough and Hagar was convinced that her son was going to die and she couldn't stand the thought of that. Any of us would not be able to stand the thought of that, none of us would want to watch a child of ours suffering and dying. We couldn't handle that. So she did what was natural. She separated herself and just laid down and cried her eyes out. But God kept his word. He took care of Ishmael and Hagar.

Now, it does seem like an odd text for Father's Day, doesn't it? It seems like a very uncomfortable text for Father's Day. It's not exactly an inspiring text on how to be a good dad, how to be a responsible parent, anything of that sort. But there's more to this story that we need to see because we look at this and we think okay there's been this family split between a father and a son. However it was that the son came to him is irrelevant because that relationship is still father and son and we read this and we think there's a irreparable split that has taken place, but we don't know the rest of the story. We miss the rest of the story. I didn't even realize this until a short while ago. Let me jump ahead with you. Remember how I always say text without context is pretext? The context of this whole story can be found in the 25th chapter of Genesis and let me just read this short little passage for you. *Then Abraham breathed his last and died at a good old age, an old man and full of years; and he was gathered to his people. His sons Isaac and Ishmael buried him in the cave of Machpelah near Mamre.* His sons Isaac and Ishmael buried him in the land of his fathers. Now, you have to realize what that one simple sentence means to this story. You see, nowadays you know if there's a split in the family and somebody dies, we swallow our pride, we make a phone call, we invite them to come for the services, come to the viewing, come to the burial, whatever. We have that ability - we'll text them, we'll send them an e-mail, we'll pick up the phone and we'll try to redeem the situation. But that's not how it would have been back then. Remember when we last left off with this story, Isaac lived here, Ishmael lived there. Somehow or another they kept in touch. Somehow or another they remained as brothers. Somehow or another there must have been some relationship there because in those days, (a) you didn't have the communication that you have now. If somebody lived a distance away, it might be a month, it might be two months that you get word of them, they can get back and be there and so on. It was not like what we have nowadays by any stretch of the imagination. So they had to be in touch, they had to be in communication, they had to be close enough to each other. And (b) the second thing is in those days you didn't have embalming, you didn't have cremation, you didn't have the things we have now. When somebody died, you buried them right way. You had generally speaking less than 24 hours between the time of death to when they were buried. Ishmael had to be there, he had to be there.

There's so much separateness in the world today. In so many ways we have this tendency to divide one from another. In the Arab Israeli story, here we have the two parties, the sons of Ishmael and the sons of Isaac. Both can claim this as their heritage - the sons of Abraham, brothers. Not as combatants one with another but as brothers together honoring their father. We human beings have this tendency to divide up, to set apart, to make delineations, to make separations, to find what makes us different rather than what makes us the same. The story of Isaac and Ishmael is a story for us today. No matter what divides us, we still need to recognize each other as brothers and sisters. It's as simple as that. It's as difficult as that. But this story of two brothers ought to be a guide and an inspiration for all of us in this time of division and strife in our world. Would you pray with me?

Ever-loving God, you have shown us the way. The path is not always easy; it was not easy for Hagar and Ishmael and it certainly could not be easy for Isaac and Sarah and Abraham, but yet, reconciliation took place. Brothers found one another. O heavenly Father help us to be your people of reconciliation in this world today. Help us to show the pathway of love and grace and mercy in a world that so desperately needs to hear some good news. We pray this in Jesus' name and for his sake, Amen.

God Will Provide?
Genesis 22: 1-14

June 28, 2020

Our text for today is from the book of Genesis, the book of beginnings. It's a story out of Abraham's life. It's one that many of you are familiar with because of its profundity, its depths of what is happening in this story, one that has caused a lot of thought over the years as to what it means and how it is that we relate to it or how it is that we ought to understand it. And it is one that has brought a lot of discomfort to some people but brought a lot of comfort to other people. Let's take a look at this story from the 22nd Chapter of Genesis, the first 14 verses there.

"Sometime later God tested Abraham. He said to him, "Abraham!". "Here I am," he replied. Then God said, "Take your son, your only son Isaac, whom you love, and go to the region of Moriah. Sacrifice him there as a burnt offering on one of the mountains I will tell you about."

Early the next morning Abraham got up and saddled his donkey. He took with him two of his servants and his son Isaac. When he had cut enough wood for the burnt offering, he set out for the place God had told him about. On the third day Abraham looked up and saw the place in the distance. He said to his servants, "Stay here with the donkey while I and the boy go over there. We will worship and then we will come back to you."

Abraham took the wood for the burnt offering and placed it on his son Isaac, and he himself carried the fire and the knife. As the two of them went on together, Isaac spoke up and said to his father Abraham, "Father?"

"Yes, my son?" Abraham replied.

"The fire and wood are here," Isaac said, "but where is the lamb for the burnt offering?"

Abraham answered, "God himself will provide the lamb for the burnt offering my son." And the two of them went on together.

When they reached the place God had told him about, Abraham built an altar there and arranged the wood on it. He bound his son Isaac and laid him on the altar, on the top of the wood. Then he reached out his hand and took the knife to slay his son. But the angel of the Lord called out to him from heaven, "Abraham! Abraham!"

"Here I am," he replied.

"Do not lay a hand on the boy," he said. "Do not do anything to him. Now I know that you fear God, because you have not withheld from me your son, your only son."

Abraham looked up and there in a thicket he saw a ram caught by its horns. He went over and took the ram and sacrificed it as a burnt offering instead of his son. So Abraham called that place The Lord Will Provide. And to this day it is said, "On the mountain of the Lord it will be provided." May the Lord bless this a portion from His holy word.

That is some story, isn't it? Can you imagine yourself in that situation? Can you imagine yourself as Abraham given that dilemma, given that situation to find yourself in? Can you imagine what Abraham might have been thinking in his mind, what might have been going through his head? What was it that Abraham was thinking? I mean it was a long trip. The Bible tells us it was three days out before they got to the base of Mount Moriah. That is an awful lot of time to do some pretty serious thinking. I mean they didn't have car radios, they didn't have tape decks, they didn't have anything but each other for conversation along the way. I can't imagine what Abraham must have been feeling like, what he must have been thinking about on those three long arduous days. But somehow or another he managed to do that journey. He managed to get himself to take everything that he needed to sacrifice his son. He managed to put one foot in front of the other to make that trip to fulfill what he heard God saying to him.

Now, the writer of Genesis uses the phrase that God tested Abraham. Well, there is a certain truth to that is there not? There is a certain truth that God was testing Abraham, "How strong is your faith? How much do you trust me? How much are you willing to do because I asked you to do it?" That's a testing. That is a way to find out whether or not Abraham truly believed God, truly trusted God at his word. Now, you have to remember that Abraham failed some tests before this time. It was, as you recall, Abraham and Sarah who never quite trusted that God would keep his word that they would have a son. And you remember from last week's sermon how that created complications and all sorts of difficulties and strife and stress in their lives because they didn't just simply trust God. So Abraham has already failed once. Abraham had already fully shown that he did not trust God. This test is almost like a final exam for him. This test is one more time for Abraham to prove his worth and his value as God's chosen one to bring God's Word into this world. To be the father of the people that God chose to reveal Himself time, and time and time again to the fullest conclusion in his self-revelation in Jesus Christ, as son of Abraham.

As we hear the story it's inspiring to us because Abraham shows more faith than I would imagine any of us in this room would have. I know I would have argued with God, I would have dragged my feet, I would have come up with 100 excuses why I couldn't make that trip, I would have put this off and put that off and put the other off, hoping that God would forget about it. I would move on from there because I would not have had the faith that Abraham had. That is part of the message here. It is setting Abraham up for us as an example of absolute faith, absolute trust in God and it's inspired a lot of beautiful artwork over the years. Because art is the way we express what our hearts know. If you traveled with me up to New Jersey (not that anybody wants to travel to New Jersey), in my mind if you had traveled with me up to New Jersey, up to the campus of Princeton University, just a hundred yards or so from the magnificent chapel on that campus is a beautiful statue of Abraham with his knife drawn and his son Isaac tied down on a pile of wood.

It's a beautiful statue. It's that kind of inspiration that this passage gives to us, that inspiration of having absolute faith.

You see though, there's actually two tests that are going on in this passage. God (for the lack of a better way to term it) is testing Abraham, but if you think about it, at the same time Abraham is testing God. How did Abraham answer when Isaac said, "you know dad, great trip, happy to go along with you but didn't we forget something? Where's the lamb? "And how did Abraham reply? He said, "Got it covered son. God will provide. "You see, there were two tests going on here. God was testing Abraham but Abraham was testing God. The trust that he had in God was being put to the test. It was a trust that God would fulfill the promises that God has made. Abraham was testing God because in the back of his mind Abraham had to remember that the same God who promised that he would have a son also promised him that his offspring would be so innumerable, that they would number more than the stars. Abraham was testing that promise from God because Abraham had to know in the back of his mind, "I can't have innumerable offspring, my legacy cannot go into innumerable number of people if it stops with the death of my son. "

Abraham's faith was based in God's word, God's promises. He knew God kept his word. It took him a while, we know that. It took him a while to get to that point before he absolutely trusted God because he didn't trust him early on (we've got the whole Ishmael thing going) but he knew at this point in his life that God's promises are sure and true. With God a promise made, is a promise kept. So Abraham was testing that theory out, testing God while God was testing him and God did provide. He sent the angels to spare Isaac, sent a ram to be offered as the sacrifice on that mountain.

Faith and trust take time. They take vision backwards in order to look forward. Abraham was able to look back on his own life and see how God had made a promise and that remarkable promise was fulfilled. And looking back, he could look forward and say that the same God who kept his word then will keep his word now.

Friends, there seems to be a lot of uncertainty in the world around us. It seems as if change is the only thing that is a constant right now. Change all around us, I mean who would ever thought that I would be wearing one of these silly things (mask). Who ever thought that you would be sitting the way that you're sitting in here. Who would have thought than many of you would be constrained to stay at home for your health and safety and well-being. So many things, so different but yet, if we look back we can see how God's promises have been sure and true. And not just the Biblical promises that we read about, promises that God made to Abraham and to so many others in the generations that followed him, promises that have been fulfilled. But in our own lives we can see time and time again how God has provided for us, how God has gotten us through challenging times in our lives, through difficult situations in our lives. How God was present there with and for us and we look back and we can see God carried us through those times but now looking back we can look forward and know that God is there with us and for us and is going to carry us through this time in which you and I find ourselves. Maybe God is testing us. But maybe it's time for us to test God as well, to trust him, to throw our lives into his care and to find in him the hope that we need for the living of our lives in the here and the now. Would you pray with me?

Our heavenly Father you are ever faithful. You have never failed us. We have failed you. We have tripped up, we have fallen, we have gotten off the path, we have wandered away, but you are ever faithful. O heavenly Father help us to look back in our lives to see the myriad of ways you have been there with us and for us and led us, O Lord, use those recollections to look forward with faith and trust and confidence. We pray this in Jesus' name. Amen.

Designing Love
Genesis 24: 34-38, 42-49, 58-67

July 5, 2020

We're continuing in our series of sermons that are coming to us out of the book of Genesis, the book of beginnings, the book of our heritage and our tradition; that tradition upon which our whole faith is based and we look today at a transition that takes place. It is a transition from one generation to another. (Now I know it's the 4th of July weekend, I should be doing something about that; please don't try to find the 4th of July in this passage. I'll just give you fair warning.) The 24th chapter of Genesis, I don't want to read the whole chapter so we have these selected verses and this is taking place in the context of Abraham sending a servant of his to go and find a suitable wife for his son Isaac. Not how we do things now a days but it was not an unusual situation in these times in which Abraham and Isaac and Sarah were living. So let's pick up in the 24th chapter with the 34th verse.

"So he said, "I am Abraham's servant. The Lord has blessed my master abundantly, and he has become wealthy. He has given him sheep and cattle, silver and gold, menservants and maid servants, and camels and donkeys. My master's wife Sarah has borne him a son in her old age, and he has given him everything he owns. And my master made me swear an oath, and said 'You must not get a wife for my son from the daughters of the Canaanites, in whose land I live, but go to my father's family and to my own clan, and get a wife for my son. ""

When I came to the spring today, I said, 'O Lord, God of my master Abraham, if you will, please grant success to the journey on which I have come. See, I am standing beside this spring; if a maiden comes out to draw water and I say to her, "Please let me drink a little water from your jar," and if she says to me, "Drink, and I'll draw water for your camels too," let her be the one the Lord has chosen for my master's son. "Before I finished praying in my heart, Rebekah came out with her jar on her shoulder. She went down to the spring and drew water, and I said to her, 'Please give me a drink.' "She quickly lowered her jar from her shoulder and said, 'Drink, and I'll water your camels too. 'So I drank and she watered the camels also. "I asked her, 'Whose daughter are you? "She said, 'The daughter of Bethuel son of Nahor, whom Milcah bore to him. '

"Then I put the ring in her nose and the bracelets on her arms, and I bowed down and worshiped the Lord. I praised the Lord, the God of my master Abraham, who had led me on the right road to get the granddaughter of my master's brother for his son. Now if you will show kindness and faithfulness to my master, tell me; and if not, tell me so I may know which way to turn. "

So they called Rebekah and asked her, "Will you go with this man? " "I will go," she said. So they sent their sister Rebekah on her way, along with her nurse and Abraham's servant and his men. And they blessed Rebekah and said to her,

> *"Our sister, may you increase to thousands upon thousands;*
> *may your offspring possess the gates of their enemies. "*

Then Rebekah and her maids got ready and mounted their camels and went back with the man. So the servant took Rebekah and left.

Now Isaac had come from Beer LahaiRoi, for he was living in the Negev. He went out to the field one evening to meditate, and as he looked up, he saw camels approaching. Rebekah also looked up and saw Isaac. She got down from her camel and asked the servant, "Who is that man in the field coming to meet us? " "He is my master," the servant answered. So she took her veil and covered herself. Then the servant told Isaac all he had done. Isaac brought her into the tent of his mother Sarah, and he married Rebekah. So she became his wife, and he loved her; and Isaac was comforted after his mother's death. 'May the Lord bless this a portion from his holy word.

We are in a whole other world with this story are we not? Everything about it is so foreign to us, so different to us, so removed from our own way of thinking and from our own experiences. There were times when my kids were young, in their teen years doing all sorts of, you know, things going on and I kind of wished we had more of a say in their lives then we actually did. There were times where I think it would have made Debby and me happy if we have just picked a spouse for them. It would have made our lives easier, cut out a lot of this falderal that goes on, you know with broken hearts and all that sort of good stuff, we would have liked to been in a culture where we could just solve the problem for our kids. It's not how we live. That's not how we do things in this day and age. We raise our children in a manner that we hope they will find the right and appropriate person who will bring them joy and happiness in their lives. That's how we do it. The trial and error of all that, the broken hearts that come and go, it's just part of it in our time, in our culture and in our way.

But in Abraham's day you didn't leave things to chance like that. And Abraham had the added burden. He knew that God had made a promise to him. God had promised to him that his children would be more than the stars so Abraham knew if that was going to be true, there's only one route to get there and that was through Isaac and Isaac better have a wife so that he can have a ton of kids and his kids can have a ton of kids and so on. Abraham had that burden on him that he had a responsibility to fulfill God's promise. Now remember too, remember too that this promise was not a promise for Abraham's sake. It was not a promise for Isaac's sake. It was not a promise for any one individual's sake or any one family's sake. The promise entailed the fact that these people would become a blessing to all people. They would become a blessing to the world. So Abraham knew that his responsibility was to see that not only the next generation carried on with his name and his traditions, with his faith and so on, but he had a responsibility for hundreds of generations yet to come. A responsibility for those hundreds of generations to be able to know and to understand who the one true God is and to be able to see and to enjoy and experience the blessings that that one true God offers. So this was no small task. This had little or nothing to do with what you and I now a days would call love or falling in love or any of those sorts of things. This had everything to do with being faithful to God, to a God who had been faithful to Abraham time and time and time again even when Abraham was less than faithful time and time and time again.

So he sent this servant out and he was a prayerful servant, did you notice that? This servant, as he was trying to fulfill his master's wishes, (you know there's no record of Abraham telling his servant now pray that God will reveal the right person you) he prays. Abraham simply gives the instructions, "go and bring back an appropriate wife for my son. "Pretty broad parameters. Not a whole lot of specificity there. But this servant ends up praying and saying "show me the right person. Show me the right woman for me to bring back. " And he challenged God with a test. He said, "I'll tell you what. I'll look for the right person that you want me to take back for my master Isaac but I'll have you show me by testing the first girl that comes along and if she responds correctly then we'll go from there. "And then Rebekah comes along doing her responsibility of bringing water back for the family and he tests her and says, "can I have a drink? "And she answers not only with the affirmative, "yes, here have a drink of water. You must be hot and tired. " But she says, "I'll take care of your livestock as well. I'll take care of your camels for you. "And right then and there the servant knew that this was the woman that God had chosen for Isaac.

I mean it's a remarkable story when you think about it. You know, her day started with going to pick up some water. . . Can you imagine? You go to the grocery store to pick something up and you never come home because somebody's taken you a million miles away because God said that's what you're supposed to do. You send a message back and it's about all you get to do with your family. But Rebekah heard the call. She listened to that call upon her life and she willingly went along and apparently what we read it must have been love at first sight between Rebekah and Isaac.

You know there's so much in this story. I mean the one thing we do know is that Abraham is getting worried about Isaac not having a wife but I think part of it was Abraham wanted Sarah to be able to die knowing that her son was taken care of because they went into her tent and had the wedding there and it's recorded that they were great comfort to Abraham after Sarah died which must not have been too long afterwards.

This is a story that helps us to see and to understand how God has worked so hard throughout the many generations in order to redeem us, to reconcile us, to keep us as a part of his family, to reveal himself a little bit at a time. As you read through the pages of the Old Testament you see the story of who God is unfolding a little bit at a time. And then you see the full revelation of God in his son, Jesus Christ, a descendent through a long line from Rebekah and Isaac.

God is so faithful to us. No matter what happens, all of the ups and downs, the ins and outs, the good and the bad that life throws upon us, the one whom we can always count upon is the Lord our God. God's faithfulness to us is there every step along the way through the good times, through the bad times, through the ups, through the downs, God is there with us and for us.

We celebrate communion, this Lord's Supper, as a reminder to us of the faithfulness of God. The length to which he goes to provide for us, to care for us, to redeem us, to restore us, to reconcile us. We take these two very simple, very common elements as reminders of God's willingness to die in his son, Jesus Christ as an ultimate act of love. In a very real sense as we saw Rebekah and Isaac falling in love as their eyes met, we celebrate this meal and the recognition that the moment that God saw us in our birth, he fell in love with us and he is willing to do anything, anything to have us be his sons and daughters. God is faithful from generation to generation to generation even when we're not faithful, God is still faithful to us. Would you pray with me?

O heavenly Father, words can never express our gratitude for the faithfulness you have shown to us in your son, Jesus Christ; for the faithfulness you have exhibited generation to generation over these many thousands of years always reaching out to us, always seeking us, always wanting us to be your faithful sons and daughters. We give you thanks through the name of Jesus Christ who alone is our Lord and Savior. Amen.

Broken Spirits, Broken Bodies
Romans 8: 1-14

July 12, 2020

Our scripture lesson today is taken from the Book of Romans and we find ourselves in that wonderful 8th chapter of Romans. A chapter that is just full of goodness and truth and mercy and love. Just absolutely full of so much good and I know I've talked before about counted cross stitch verses, verses that you want to have displayed in your house to see, to be reminded and this would be kind of a counted cross stitch chapter. You put the whole chapter up on the wall to see it and use it, to remind you of how God works with us and for us. So let's take a look at Romans Chapter 8 and we'll start with the first 11 verses.

Therefore, there is now no condemnation for those who are in Christ Jesus, because through Christ Jesus the law of the Spirit of life set me free from the law of sin and death. For what the law was powerless to do in that it was weakened by the sinful nature, God did by sending his own Son in the likeness of sinful man to be a sin offering. And so he condemned sin in sinful man, in order that the righteous requirements of the law might be fully met in us who do not live according to the sinful nature but according to the Spirit.

Those who live according to the sinful nature have their minds set on what that nature desires; but those who live in accordance with the Spirit have their minds set on what the Spirit desires. The mind of sinful man is death, but the mind controlled by the Spirit is life and peace; the sinful mind is hostile to God. It does not submit to God's law, nor can it do so. Those controlled by the sinful nature cannot please God.

You, however, are controlled not by the sinful nature but by the Spirit, if the Spirit of God lives in you. And if anyone does not have the Spirit of Christ, he does not belong in Christ. But if Christ is in you, your body is dead because of sin, yet your spirit is alive because of righteousness. And if the Spirit of him who raised Jesus from the dead is living in you, he who raised Christ from the dead will also give life to your mortal bodies through his Spirit, who lives in you. May the Lord bless this a portion from his holy word.

It's a wonderful passage, is it not? It is one that is filled with hope. In Christ there is no condemnation. That's pretty good news I'd say. It's awfully good news you'd have to say. It is a proclamation of God's absolute love for each and every one of us. The law of God is set aside and the grace of God has taken prominence. That's great news! That's good for us to hear! That's good for us to know about! It's good for us to be able to live our lives knowing that no matter how far we have fallen short of who God has called us to be, we cannot be condemned for those failures. Those failures are not held against us. But how does that live out in our lives? What is Paul trying to say to us in these first 11 verses of the 8th chapter of Romans? What is it that he wants his readers to know and to understand about what it means to live as ones who are no longer under condemnation; no longer having our sins accounted to us? How is it that we live as one for whom the slate has been cleaned?

Paul is concerned. Paul is concerned and you can hear it in some of the language that he uses because Paul is talking about the spirit and the body as he goes through these verses here, as he goes through this section of his letter to the church at Rome. He keeps on making it a contrast between the body and the spirit and we oftentimes, I think, misunderstand that and Paul does not want us to misunderstand that. We oftentimes slip from Christ to Plato and we don't even realize we're doing it. The Platonic way of thinking is an undergirding way of our philosophy of looking at the world. There's so much that we think about and I believe we don't think about it, it's just part of who we are, it's become ingrained in our culture. One of the fallacies of Plato that Paul is fighting against here is the fallacy that what is physical is evil and what is spiritual is good. But Paul does not want us to think that way and that has crept back into our minds over the generations and we oftentimes think of that phrase "there is no condemnation in Christ" as being a simple statement of what happens when we die. We think of it as a simple statement that says when you die and you get to the pearly gates and St. Peter meets you there and he checks out the book and he says, "Oh look, you're a Christian, come on in. "And we think that is all that it means - that our slate has been cleaned, you've got a clean bill of eternal health and we're ready to go but we forget there's a lot of time between here and eternity, whether it's 24 hours, 24 years or 240 years who knows. Medicine is improving every year. Maybe soon we'll have life expectancies well over 100 years. We don't know, we hope and pray but we have this idea that this life is irrelevant in many ways and that what Christ has done for us is for that time, for that day out there. I'm not saying it is and I'm not saying that this isn't about what Christ has done for us for eternity but Paul wants us to see that it is about today as well. That when we live in the love of Jesus Christ, that starts here and now, that starts today and is a part of who we are each and every day.

I have a friend who has on more than one occasion has said to me, "I hate it when I read in the obituaries where it says such and such has gone to be with the Lord. "He says, "Isn't the truth that they're with the Lord every day of their lives and the Lord is with us every day of our lives? " And that's precisely right. That's what Paul is trying to say to us! The here and now means something. It is not all about the here and after. It's about the here and now and how it is that we live as forgiven people. The first thing we have to do is get out of our minds, get out of our heads that this physical world is not something good. Wasn't it God who looked at what he created and his assessment was it is good? That has not changed.

One of the things that perturbs the heck out of me is conversations that I've had with some people who like to say that they are deeply spiritual people. They don't go to church, they don't believe in most anything and when I follow up and I ask them, "what do you mean that you are spiritual, that you're a deeply spiritual person? " They usually say something along the lines of "well I like to go to the ocean and when I stare out at the ocean and I consider the vastness of it; it's a very spiritual experience for me. "Or they might say, "I love to go to the Blue Ridge Parkway and I love to watch the sun setting and that's a very spiritual experience for me. "And I think that's fine. Those are wonderful experiences. I love being at the ocean, I love being in the mountains, I love watching a beautiful sunset and Debby will tell you that oftentimes when I see a beautiful sunset (and it drives her crazy) I'll applaud "author, author", giving thanks to God for the creation of such beauty.

However, what Paul is trying to help us to see is that as those who are no longer condemned, as ones who now seek to live guided by the very spirit of God, the Holy Spirit living within us, living through us, that true spirituality is now seen not as crossing T's, dotting I's in the laws, but true spirituality is seen in the way that we love one another. That maybe, maybe the most spiritual acts we can do are showing kindness to others. Just the other night, Debby and I were out, we went to the donut shop for a donut, but as we made the turn to the corner where the donut shop was, there was a poor fellow sitting there looking bedraggled, skinny as a rail, probably looking older than he actually was. We pulled into the donut shop, there at Krispy Kreme on Broad Street, Debby remembered that we had in the back of our car a little bag that had a gift card to McDonald's, a bottle of water and a few other things to help somebody out. And so, she being the real Christian in the family, remembered that, took the bag and went and gave it to that man and he was so grateful, so grateful for that simple act of kindness.

You see, living by the Spirit, living by the guidance of the Holy Spirit, living as people who no longer stand under the condemnation of the law, we find our true Spirit, true existence taking shape and form in the world in which we live. We allow the Spirit to move in our hearts and our lives when we are touched by someone else's need and we're able to meet that need. It could just be as simple listening to somebody tell you their problems. It could be as simple as making an apple pie and taking it to somebody who just needs some cheering up. It could be as simple as picking up the telephone and calling someone who, for whatever reason, was on your heart just to check up on them to see how they're doing.

The other day I was able to take some help that you all have given to the church for me to assist people in need in this COVID-19 pandemic, I didn't think it was very much and I didn't know if it was going to help at all, but when I gave that simple gift card to that man and he started to cry, I knew what Paul was talking about. The Spirit moved in your hearts to give a little extra just for the purpose of helping those who are in need. The Spirit moved in my heart to think of this person and to listen to their story, to understand their situation. That's what Paul is talking about here. That we who live as ones who are no longer condemned, no longer have to live under the law, no longer do we have to worry about crossing the T's and dotting the I's but we are given the blessing of living our lives under the guidance of the Holy Spirit. To show the spirit within us through our acts of love and compassion. You see, Plato had it all wrong. Plato didn't get it at all. This life is good. This life is worth enjoying. This life is worth cherishing. This life is worth everything because we have been redeemed as part of the kingdom. Not some day in the great by and by, but now, here, in this time, in this situation, we are called to share his love through our hearts and through our lives. And when we practice love, when we practice kindness, we're truly, truly being spiritual. Would you pray with me?

Almighty and ever-loving God, we thank you that because of the love your son, Jesus Christ, because of his sacrifice for us, we can live as people who are no longer under condemnation and we can live as forgiven people allowing your love to fill our hearts to overflowing. Help us always to see how it is that we can draw closest to you when we are kindest to others. We pray this in Jesus' name, Amen.

Labor Pains
Romans 8: 12 - 25

July 19, 2020

Our text for today is taken from the book of Romans in the 8th chapter, 12-25 verses there as we continue our study of Romans in these few weeks together. Let me just jump into it.

Therefore brothers, we have an obligation - but it is not to the sinful nature, to live according to it. For if you live according to the sinful nature, you will die; but if by the Spirit you put to death the misdeeds of the body, you will live, because those who are led by the Spirit of God are sons of God. For you did not receive a spirit that makes you a slave again to fear, but you received the Spirit of sonship. And by him we cry, "Abba, Father."The Spirit himself testifies with our spirit that we are God's children. Now if we are children, then we are heirs - heirs of God and co-heirs with Christ, if indeed we share in his sufferings in order that we may also share in his glory.

I consider that our present sufferings are not worth comparing with the glory that will be revealed in us. The creation waits in eager expectation for the sons of God to be revealed. For the creation was subjected to frustration, not by its own choice, but by the will of the one who subjected it, in hope that the creation itself will be liberated from its bondage to decay and brought into the glorious freedom of the children of God.

We know that the whole creation has been groaning as in the pains of childbirth right up to the present time. Not only so, but we ourselves, who have the firstfruits of the Spirit, groan inwardly as we wait eagerly for our adoption as sons, the redemption of our bodies. For in this hope we were saved. But hope that is seen is no hope at all. Who hopes for what he already has? But if we hope for what we do not yet have, we wait for it patiently. May the Lord bless this a portion from his holy word.

Again as we go through this 8th chapter of Romans, it is a chapter chocked full of so much good stuff and I can't really do it justice even in these few short verses, twelve or thirteen verses that we just read together today. There is so much in there for us to ponder and consider. I want us to take a look at the tail end of this, that's kind of the summation that Paul is offering to us of what he is trying to say. Paul talks in the end there about hope and he talks about how we are part of creation and that all of God's creation is groaning inwardly as if in the pangs of childbirth, as we eagerly await our body's redemption. Now that's an interesting use of different imagery. It's an interesting way of looking at what God is doing in this world in and through us and sometimes we don't quite see it as clearly as we ought to.

What is Paul trying to make sure that we see and we understand in this passage? Now first of all, I'm not sure why the apostle Paul uses the imagery that he uses that we are in the pangs of childbirth. I don't think any man should ever write about the pangs of childbirth. I don't think that we are allowed to claim we know anything about it. Debby would tell you that I am absolutely oblivious to it because when she was giving birth to Chad, Dr. Charlie Meekle was the physician, he and I were standing off to the side while Debby was in the pangs of childbirth and we were having this wonderful conversation. He had been a medical doctor in the army, I was a chaplain in the air force, so we were swapping stories about what it was like in our respective military duties when Debby ever so quietly, ever so gently spoke up and said, "would one of you mind paying some attention to me?" I don't think it was me she wanted but I went over anyway. I know what side my bread is buttered on. We'll just leave it at that. So I don't know why Paul would use such an analogy for us since it is a foreign experience to him and to any man in particular, but anyone who had never given birth to a child, it's a bit of a foreign analogy. Paul usually uses good analogies that most of us can relate clearly and well to. But the only thing I can think of here is that he is trying to help us to see something. He's trying to help us understand that no matter what our present sufferings are, what is coming ahead is beyond our ability to comprehend it's goodness. The pangs of childbirth leads to the beauty of the birth of a child. I'll never forget, I'll always remember when each of my kids were born and what a wonderful experience that was and was beyond my comprehension: the beauty, the joy, and the happiness of those moments. I was so caught up in it. I'll be honest with you when Courtney was born, our older child, the doctor takes her, wraps her all up and says, "well let's see what we have here" and I'm thinking well that's a dumb question, it's a baby what do you think it is. I was so caught up in the moment I forgot there were two choices. I thought it could be a boy or a girl - I forgot about that. But it was such an overwhelming moment and overwhelming experience that I was just caught up in the beauty and the happiness and joy of that moment. I think that's what Paul is trying to get across to us - that no matter how difficult things are, no matter how trying times may be, no matter how tired you and I are of living in a COVID-19 world, no matter how tired you and I are living in a time of unrest, living in a time of political conflict, living in a time when you have to be so careful what you say for fear of being misinterpreted, no matter how tired we are of everything that seems to be weighing down upon us in these days, no matter how difficult a situation may be that we are going through either personally or in the grand scheme of things, we live as people of hope - that God is going to bring something good out of it. That's why Paul used that analogy. That's why Paul used that analogy so that we would have some comprehension in our mind that as difficult, as challenging, as painful as life might be to us, God is working for good for each one of us.

But there's another part in here. There's another part in here that oftentimes we miss and we misunderstand. There's that phrase that Paul uses, he says, "What we eagerly await, the redemption of our bodies. We slip again into a path that somehow says this life is miserable but someday I'm going to die and go to heaven and everything will be perfect. We tend to make this dichotomy between the misery of this life and the beauty of the next life and that's a false dichotomy. That's not what Paul is saying here. He's not talking about eagerly awaiting the day I get to die! You know that's not Paul. You've heard him elsewhere talking about what he still wants to accomplish, what he wants to do, what he wants to get done. He loved life in it's fullest! He was always trying to do more, say more, be with more people, experience more of God's grace and love in his life. What he's saying here is he's making an analogy in his mind there's life of the spirit and the life of the body, the life of the spirit, the life of flesh. He constantly uses this analogy in his writings. He's constantly makes contrasts and comparisons between the two. But he's not saying the spirit going to heaven is the goal, that the body, the life of the flesh is bad. What he's trying to say is that we need to have a life that is controlled by the spirit. We need to live a life that has been redeemed: our goals in life are now changed and refocused. No longer as followers of Jesus Christ do we live for ourselves, for our own desires, our own good, our own game but we live our lives led by the Spirit within us. So when Paul is talking about "we eagerly await the redemption of our bodies," he's taking about eagerly desiring, eagerly awaiting God's taking full control over our lives in the here and the now helping us become the people we were created to be. Helping us become true sons and daughters of God, true heirs, true ones who have received fully God's love, grace and mercy in our lives so that our lives reflect that love and mercy. So that people no longer see we ourselves, but they begin to see Christ living in and through us. That we have become redeemed as human beings, that we are doing his work and his will in this world.

You see Paul is trying to, he's trying to encourage the church in a time when there were a lot of other troubles, trials and tribulations. If you think we have it rough by having to wear a mask, if you think we have it rough by trying not to shake hands when you want to shake hands so desperately, you think we have it rough because we can't hug people the way we would love to hug them, it's nothing compared to what the early church was enduring. They were undergoing persecution, being killed, being persecuted, being beaten, all sorts of horrible things were happening to people who said I'm a follower of Jesus Christ. And Paul is trying to write to the church in that context, in that time and give them a word of encouragement, not to say, "boy I can't wait to get to heaven," but instead for them to see that they have heaven here and now in their lives. A glimpse of it, a participation in it, that once the love of God truly touches our hearts and our minds, that we begin to be changed, we begin to be redeemed, we begin to become truly spiritual people living our lives not for ourselves but for the glory of God in our love of others. Paul wants us to have that encouragement no matter what travail we might be enduring, no matter how discouraged we might get, no matter how difficult our lives might seem, God is working in and through us redeeming us to be his people to show his love in this time and in this situation. Would you pray with me?

O God of grace and God of mercy, we do give you thanks for your never ending love, your ever presence with us in each of our lives. We thank O Lord that even as we are gathered today, even as we are hearing your word, even as we are praying, you are redeeming us, changing us, helping us to live our lives in the manner that you would have us live them. We give you thanks O Lord for that hope, that hope in you, that hope in what you are doing in and through us. We give you thanks for the name of Jesus Christ who alone is our Lord and our Savior. Amen.

Inseparable
Romans 8: 26 - 39

July 26, 2020

Our scripture for this morning brings us to the end of the 8th chapter of Paul's letter to the church at Rome. And as I said earlier on that the 8th chapter of Romans is kind of a counted cross-stitch chapter. If you were to have the space in your house and you wanted to have some words on the wall that would offer you comfort, encourage, hope, perspective, the 8th chapter of Romans would be that chapter to put on your wall. And now as we get into the 26-39th verses, we really get into those passages which are very familiar to us, words that are just so comforting and encouraging. Words that we need so much as we go through these challenging times in our lives, in our community and in our nation, so we read in the 8th chapter beginning with the 26th verse, 26-39:

In the same way, the Spirit helps us in our weakness. We do not know what we ought to pray for but the Spirit himself intercedes for us with groans that words cannot express. And he who searches our hearts knows the mind of the Spirit, because the Spirit intercedes for the saints in accordance with God's will.

And we know that in all things God works for the good of those who love him, who have been called according to his purpose. For those God foreknew he also predestined to be conformed to the likeness of his Son, that he might be the firstborn among many brothers. And those he predestined, he also called; those he called, he also justified; those he justified, he also glorified.

What, then, shall we say in response to this? If God is for us, who can be against us? He who did not spare his own Son, but gave him up for us all - how will he not also, along with him, graciously give us all things? Who will bring any charge against those whom God has chosen? It is God who justifies. Who is he that condemns? Christ Jesus, who died - more than that, who was raised to life - is at the right hand of God and is also interceding for us. Who shall separate us from the love of Christ? Shall trouble or hardship or persecution or famine or nakedness or danger or sword? As it is written:

> "For your sake we face death all day long;
> we are considered as sheep to be slaughtered."

Now, in all these things we are more than conquerors through him who loved us. For I am convinced that neither death nor life, neither angels nor demons, neither the present nor the future, nor any powers, neither height nor depth, nor anything else in all creation, will be able to separate us from the love of God that is in Christ Jesus our Lord. May the Lord bless this a portion from his holy word.

Doing things that are challenging and doing them alone is very difficult. Nobody likes to do something that is difficult or challenging when you are all by yourself. That's why whenever we are going through a challenging situation, going through a challenging time, we like to have those people who are with us, or those people whom we love with us to get us through those challenging times. If we were to have surgery or some medical procedure that was very frightening, what we would want is to have somebody with us to hold our hand, to offer us words of encouragement, to just be there even without a word being spoken, just to have them there, to have that presence with us would make it so much easier and so much better for us. To do things alone is difficult and we do get anxious, we do get nervous, we do get scared in situations like that.

I remember when I was a young man, I think I was 16 or 17, my dad had double booked himself on a Sunday. In the summer the churches in Carbondale PA would unite together, the three Protestant churches in town would unite together and each minister would take three weeks and the other ministers would get six weeks off. But Dad didn't like having six weeks off from the pulpit, I don't quite understand that myself, I enjoy having a few weeks away, Dad was different than I am. And so what he would do was he would volunteer himself to preach at small churches that had to rely upon guest ministers. On this particular Sunday, in the summer, he realized he had booked himself for two churches but not enough time to get between the two churches. He knew it would be a rush and so he said to me, he said, "Stephen I need you to do something for me," and I said, "Sure Dad" just like my kids always say, "Sure Dad." "I'm not sure how that conversation went now that I recall it, but anyhow Dad talked me into just leading the worship at the Union Dale Presbyterian Church (that's two words, that's how you know it's Pennsylvania and not New York. Uniondale New York is one word, Union Dale, Pennsylvania is two words. There's your trivia today if you ever get that question on a trivia game, you'll be all set.)So at the Uniondale Presbyterian Church, down in the country, one of the prettiest little country churches you ever saw, it's out in the middle of the woods there and I got there, their service started at 11, Dad was finishing up at the other church about 10:30, plenty of time for him to travel the forty-five minutes that it would take him to get between the two churches. All I had to do was just do the opening part of the service, Call to Worship, Prayer of Confession and few other traditional sorts of things. I had a prayer all written out but Dad said, just in case something happens, car breaks down or something happens and I can't get there, I want you to have a sermon ready. So I wrote out a sermon, to be prepared, and I had that ready as well. I was, well I won't say I was confident, I just thought I had everything prepared. I won't say I was confident because I was scared to death to go into that little country church even though they were the nicest bunch of folks you'd ever meet. 10, 12, 15 people just the nicest bunch of folks you'd ever meet, but I was just scared to death and I got into that pulpit and I led them in the worship, I got them through the hymns, I got them through the prayers, I got them through everything and kept looking at that door waiting to see Dad, no Dad didn't come through that door. So I pull out the little sermon that I had and treated them to the sermon, finished up the sermon and there's Dad at the door. I thought to myself how did it take him so long to get here? Where was he this whole time? Did the car break down? Did he have some troubles, what happened? Well the fact of the matter is I did an hour service in 24 minutes because I was so nervous, I talked so fast and I just did the whole service so quickly and the sermon probably was about three minutes. You'd love to see me reenact that wouldn't you?

But doing something that you are challenged with does bring out that nervousness. I'd bet you I would have done a ten times better job in leading worship that day if my Dad had been sitting there the whole time. I would have been more relaxed, I would have been more comfortable, I would have spoken at a pace that people could have understood the words that I was saying because his presence would have helped me get through that time.

This passage, in Romans chapter 8, is just that reminder for you and me. That no matter what the situation may be, no matter what we might be going through, no matter how challenging life might feel to us, no matter how concerned we are about what tomorrow might bring, no matter how frightening the situation might feel to us, no matter how much turmoil we might be feeling about what is happening around us, God is with us. God is for us. In those times in our lives when we cannot even articulate what fears we are feeling when we cannot even articulate in our prayers what is troubling us in our hearts, Paul reminds us that God is with us through the Holy Spirit and will takes those groanings, those troubles that are within us and make them understandable to God and God will understand because God is with us. When we are facing trials in our lives, when we feel as if it weren't for bad luck we'd have no luck at all (how many ministers quote Hee-Haw in their sermons - none of you are old enough to remember Hee-Haw), we're at that stage in our lives, we're at that point in our lives, we feel as if everything has been turned upside down on us, if we're in that stage in our life and that place in our life where we feel as if everything that once was certain to us is now shaky ground, we know that we have that certainty of God's love, of God's presence with us and for us in our lives. Paul runs through that wonderful litany of things. You can almost hear Paul just thinking out loud as he's scribbling this down, thinking of things that could possibly separate us from the love of God and he runs through the gamut of them. He runs through them all these things: trouble, hardship, persecution, famine, nakedness, the sword and he's just running through this list of things that we might find frightening and he says throw the worst at me, throw the worst of the worst at me and I will always know that God is with me.

Nothing, nothing in all creation can separate us from the love of God which is in Jesus Christ our Lord. If you want proof of God's presence with us, if you want proof of the distance that God would go to be with us and for us, look at the person of Jesus Christ. Look at the work of Jesus Christ. Not even the cross could keep him from loving us, not even death was more powerful than his love. It doesn't matter what the situation might be, it doesn't matter if it's concern about the future, whether it's a concern about finances, whether it's concern about family, whether it's concern about whatever it might be, there is one certainty - that's the love of God. The love of God is that rock on which you can stand. The love of God is that still point - that point of stillness that when everything else seems to be spinning out of control, the love of God is that still point. And even as Paul was writing this he's building to a crescendo in this chapter, he uses phrases like "I know, I know, I know" but when he gets to this point at the end of the chapter, he says, "I am convinced. "He's gone from just knowing something saying yes this is true, yes this is true to being convinced. You see that distinction? Do you see what Paul is saying here? That he is absolutely convinced, you could tell him a thousand other things, you could argue with him, you could say that's not true, you can say it in 100 ways and give him 1,000 examples but he is absolutely convinced that nothing in all of creation can separate us from the love of God which is in Jesus Christ our Lord.

These are trying times. I won't say otherwise. These are challenging times for every one of us. But we know that God is working good out of this and that God is there with us and for us and will get us through the most challenging times we'll ever face. Would you pray with me?

Our heavenly Father, your presence, your love is exactly what we need. For you are that ever-present help and we are so grateful. Help us to be like Paul and be so convinced that we can face anything as long as we know that you are with us. We pray this in Jesus' name. Amen.

Not the Normal Way
Romans 9: 1-5

August 2, 2020

As I have mentioned innumerable times before but I'll mention it again, that text without context is pretext and so this passage this morning we need to hear it in light of Paul's full conversation, in light of the place in which it falls as a continuation of the 8th chapter of Romans. As we recall the 8th chapter of Romans is that is just chocked full of wonderful promises and hopes and it just is absolutely full of so many good things upon which we can just grab hold and hold dearly in each of our lives. Paul has just concluded reminding us that there is nothing, absolutely nothing, he's absolutely convinced that there is nothing in all creation which can separate us from the love of God which is in Christ Jesus our Lord. He just finished reminding us of that absolute truth and so now you have to hear that passage in that context. Let's take a look at the 9th chapter of Romans; we're just going to read the first five verses. It's a pretty lengthy section but I'll just read the first five verses so you can get a feel for where Paul is now.

"I speak the truth in Christ - I am not lying, my conscience confirms it in the Holy Spirit - I have great sorrow and unceasing anguish in my heart. For I could wish that I myself were cursed and cut off from Christ for the sake of my brothers and sisters, those of my own race, the people of Israel. Theirs is the adoption as sons; theirs the divine glory, the covenants, the receiving of the law, the temple worship and the promises. Theirs are the patriarchs, and from them is traced the human ancestry of Christ, who is God over all, forever praised! Amen.' 'May the Lord bless this a portion from his holy word. (24:16)

Paul has taken a little turn here on us. It's gone from all of the wonderful promises, the good news to Paul having a heartfelt expression of his sense of loss at the Jewish community not all following in the messiahship of Jesus. He's having a heartfelt experience where he is trying to express that he doesn't really understand why so many in the Jewish faith, his brothers and sisters, those who were close friends of his who now do not see who Jesus is and what Jesus has done for all of us. He wants everyone to know the person and work of Jesus Christ. He wants everyone to know that Jesus is Lord of all, he wants everyone to know that God's love extends to every human being, he wants everyone to know that there is nothing in all creation that can separate us from that love of God which is in Jesus Christ our Lord. He wants everybody to know that, to experience that, to have that in their hearts and in their lives. That's what he is hoping for, he desperately wants that and it concerns him that the very people who should be the first ones to get it, to understand it, to comprehend it, to experience it are turning and walking away from the truth of who Jesus Christ is and what he has done. And that bothers Paul because he wants everybody to know who Jesus is and he particularly wants those whom he feels the closest to experience that in their lives as well because Paul is pointing out to us in this ninth chapter the fact that the Jewish people had every advantage given to them to know and to understand what God is doing. They had the prophets, they had the patriarchs, they had all of those historical and hereditary benefits given to them, that they are of that line and lineage of the people that God chose whose to be his bearers of good news to the world.

The very line and lineage of Jesus Christ himself is found in the Jewish people. Every advantage, every advantage they had was theirs and yet with all of that background, with all that information, with all the understanding of God's love for them over all those generations, how God's grace prevails time and time and time again, how God stood by the covenant even when his people wandered away from it, how God stood by his people when time and time again they walked in a different path than the one they were called to walk. And God took them back time and time and time again. They should have understood grace just by experience, just by their own history as a people but they didn't get it. And the stumbling block for them and this is an understandable stumbling block and it's one that still causes many people to reject Jesus to this day; and the stumbling block is this that the Jewish people truly understood the otherness of God. They knew that God was one who was wholly different than we humans are. They understood the greatness of God, they understood the otherness of God in terms of God being one who could create the world with a word. They knew their story. They knew how God could act, how God could create the world with a word; God could part the seas with a word and people could walk across dry land to escape their oppression. They knew that this God whom they loved this God whom they worshiped was somebody who was absolutely different than you and I. I can't even create something when I'm following the recipe or the instruction book and I can't even walk through cold water no less part those waters. We're all human and the Jewish people understood the distinction - that strong distinction between being human and who God is.

So if God is wholly other, if God is so different from us, the stumbling block becomes the Word became flesh and dwelt among us. The stumbling block became the thought that God could take upon himself human form, that God would need to eat and to drink, that God would need to get a decent night's sleep, that God would feel the pain of people that he trusted betraying him, that God would feel the exasperation of what it feels like to teach people over a three year period and look at them and know that they still don't get it. And they certainly couldn't understand a God who would become flesh, who could suffer and die on a cross scandalized, pain-ridden, abandoned. Those experiences were very human experiences and the Jewish people could not link together a God who is holy other with a God who would become flesh and would die on a cross. What they didn't understand was that God's ways are not our ways. That might have been part of the language but it was not a part of their understanding.

They forgot that God doesn't always play by the rules. I mean, you just take their lineage - according to the rules the first son is the one who inherits, the first son is the one who carries down the lineage, the first son is the one who has all of the responsibilities to carry on the father's work into the next generation. But God broke the rules there. Isn't it Isaac that is the for bearer and not the older Ishmael? Isn't it Jacob who is the for bearer that they follow and not Esau? You see God constantly broke the rules for the benefit of his people. God constantly broke the rules in order that his people would be able to know and to understand and to experience his love, his grace, his mercy. And in the very person of Jesus Christ, God broke the ultimate rule of God being holy other and distant and separate from us, becoming a God who walked among us, who shared our experiences, who endured the temptation, who endured the heat, who endured hunger pains, who endured friends who didn't get it. The ultimate rule being broken was that man-made rule that God is limited to being out there somewhere. The word became flesh and dwelt among us. Because God broke that rule so that we might see and experience the depth and the breath and the height of his love toward each and every one of us. God broke that rule in the person of Jesus Christ as he suffered and died upon the cross not to appease an angry God, not to do anything other than to be the ultimate act of selfless love, a selfless love that took upon himself a death upon the cross that he did not deserve in any way, shape, form or manner. An act of absolute love that we remember every time that we take some of that bread, every time we drink from those cups, we remember, we remember that God was willing to break the rules to be with us and for us. God was willing to break the rules so that we might see clearly and tangibly and understandably the depths of love that he has for every person. God broke the rules so that everyone, every nation, every tongue, every tribe, every generation might know that there is nothing in all of creation that could possibly separate us from the love of God which is in Jesus Christ our Lord. And O how Paul languished in his desire for everyone to know, to understand and to experience that love. Would you pray with me?

Our heavenly Father, your love is so incomprehensible. A love that knew no bounds that even becoming flesh and dwelling among us, even a death upon the cross, was not beyond the scope of your love through your son Jesus Christ. Even death itself was broken by the power of your love. O heavenly Father let that love fill our hearts and our lives that we are renewed and strengthened as you sons and daughters. In Jesus' name we pray, Amen.

The Math of Forgiveness
Matthew 18: 21-35

September 13, 2020

Good morning! You don't know how good it is to be here with all of you today and it's wonderful to be back home again and feeling well. I do want to say a big thank you for all of you who prayed for me while I was so sick and the truth of the matter is, I really believe this, that I started to make a turn for the better after I humbled myself enough to ask for your prayers and so I really believe your prayers made a big difference in my healing so I genuinely appreciate that your prayers along with good medical care has brought me back to being able to stand before you today and I am grateful and thankful for each of you and your ministry.

The sermon series that we are doing is an interesting one. The title of the series is "Learning How to Fight Fair" and what we're doing is taking a look at a number of passages of scripture to help us to learn how to deal better with each other within families, within communities, within society. We need to, obviously, learn how to be better people and how to live with one another in a way that is not destructive. We tend, as a society right now to lean toward the destructive; that we have seemingly lost the ability to have conversation and have dialog and have understanding and so the church needs to get back to it's roots, get back to the point where we become a people who set a better example, a better way of how to live our lives and live together. Today's passage of scripture is one that is intriguing, it's a parable that Jesus taught particularly aimed towards Peter who asked him a question and it's intriguing, it's fun, you know it's one of those ones you kind of chuckle. At the of it you go, yea that would never happen. But, the fact of the matter is, it's actually a very honest look at ourselves. Let's take a look at this of scripture from the 18th chapter of the gospel according to Matthew beginning with the 21st verse:

Then Peter came to Jesus and asked, "Lord, how many times shall I forgive my brother when he sins against me? Up to seven times?"

Jesus answered, "I tell you, not seven times, but seventy-seven times. Therefore, the kingdom of heaven is like a king who wanted to settle accounts with his servants. As he began the settlement, a man who owed him ten thousand talents was brought to him. Since he was not able to pay, the master ordered that he and his wife and his children and all that he had to be sold to repay the debt.

The servant fell on his knees before him, 'Be patient with me,' he begged, 'and I will pay back everything. The servant's master took pity on him, canceled the debt and let him go.

But when the servant went out, he found one of his fellow servants who owed him a hundred denary. He grabbed him and began to choke him. 'Pay back what you owe me!' he demanded.

His fellow servant fell to his knees and begged him, 'Be patient with me, and I will pay you back.'

But he refused. Instead, he went off and had the man thrown into prison until he could pay the debt. When the other servants saw what had happened, they were greatly distressed and went and told their master everything that had happened.

Then the master called the servant in. 'You wicked servant,' he said. 'I canceled all that debt of yours because you begged me to. Shouldn't you have had mercy on your fellow servant just as I had on you?' in anger his master turned him over to the jailers to be tortured, until he should pay back all he owed.

This is how my heavenly Father will treat each of you unless you forgive your brother from your heart.' May the Lord bless this a portion from his holy word.

I was asked a little while ago now about what is the difference between pastoral care and pastoral counseling. Aren't they the same thing? So I tried to explain that pastoral care is trying to listen, show care, compassion, think theologically, and pray with somebody. Pastoral counseling is the ability to diagnose a problem and to bring about some sort of resolution to that issue. As an example, a good number of years ago now I had a couple call me up and ask if they could come in and talk with me. They were having some struggles in their marriage and felt that they needed somebody to be a third party, somebody to just kind of listen to them and I said "sure" and set up a time, they came in and sat down, we had some nice pleasantries, talked about a number of different things and then I said, "what is it that is troubling you? What is it that is really bothering you?" And the husband said, "Well, my wife remembers everything I have ever done wrong and she always reminds me of it." Well the wife jumped right in and she said, "I do not! You always say that! Why just last week when we were at my mother's house you told her the same thing and then the other time when we were over. . . " and she went through this whole list of all the times that her husband had said that she had kept track of all the wrongs that he had done. That started out as pastoral care. I quickly shipped them off for some counseling.

But that is human nature. That is a problem that we bear as human beings. Keeping track of wrongs. Holding grudges, carrying resentments, the inability to forgive someone who has done us harm, who has done wrong to us. Peter understood that. He understood human nature and he understood that Jesus was trying to call his disciples to call his followers to a little higher standard of living, a better way to live our lives and so he went to Jesus because he wanted some simple clarification. He wanted to know how many times does he have to forgive someone. And Peter thought, "you know what? I'll show Jesus I'm a good man. I'll show Jesus that you know I can be a very gracious person." He says, 'you think seven times is enough? If I forgive him seven times can I carry a grudge from there? Would that be okay Jesus? Seven seems like a lot" and Jesus says, "No. Not seven times Peter" and there are some questions about the translation here. The translation says "not seven times but seventy-seven times." A better translation I think is actually "seventy times seven times." Now I think what Jesus was saying was that forgiveness needs to be generous, free and not counted because none of us are going to be able, you know, unless you pull up a sheet on the computer, to keep track and get that seventy times seven, that would be what 490 times? Who's going to keep track of 490 times?

Jesus was making the point that forgiveness needs to be freely given. It needs to be something that comes from our hearts. It is not measured, it is not counted, we don't keep track of it, we just freely give it. And that seems like a lot to ask. That seems like an awful lot to ask: to offer that kind of grace. And Jesus knew, he probably read Peter's face because Peter, as we know, was kind of an honest guy, what he was thinking, you knew. And probably his face just showed his shock and dismay at Jesus' answer to him.

And so, Jesus tells this parable, the story of a wealthy man who was at a point in his life where he wanted to get all of his accounts squared away and so he called in all those who were indebted to him to see how they were doing and he called in this servant of his, this employee of his and said, 'you know what? You are into me pretty deep. You owe me 10,000 denarii. "That was a ton of money. That was a debt that both the wealthy man and his employee knew would be nearly impossible to ever pay off. So, the wealthy man says, "I got to do what I got to do, I'm a businessman. I'm going to have you sell everything you own, sell your family and that will at least partially pay me back for your indebtedness" and the man fell to his knees as any of us would and begged for mercy and the rich fellow had compassion and forgave his debt. Now if the story ended there it would have been a great story. It would have been a wonderful story if it ended right there but then it takes this uncomfortable turn because this fellow goes outside and as he is walking and leaving the head office of his boss, he sees a colleague of his who owes him just a little bit of money, grabs him by the throat, begins to choke him, demands his money back and has the guy thrown into debtors prison until the debt could be made whole. Now this didn't go over well. There were people who saw this happening and they told the boss about it and the wealthy fellow says, "I can't have this" and brought the man in and said "it's not the way we do it. I forgave you 10,000 denarii and you don't have the grace to forgive 100 denarii. "An uncomfortable turn but what Jesus was trying to show was that we as his followers, we as disciples do not live as good people, we do not live as wonderful people, we do not live as people who are better than anyone else. The only thing that makes us Christians is the fact that we have been forgiven. Our debts have been wiped clean. Our sins have been erased.

In the Wyalusing Church there was a wonderful women who was a member there. She had retired from teaching speech and theater in the S. U. N. Y. system, Ellen Murphy Terrell a wonderful woman, about 5 foot tall and maybe weighed 50-60 pounds, she was just a little might mite. But she had the most magnificent speaking voice you ever heard which was wonderful, 99% of the time. But in that 1% of the time was when she was doing a little protest as we would do The Lord's Prayer every Sunday as we would say forgive us our debts as we forgive our debtors, she would say forgive us our trespasses as we forgive those who trespass against us and she would say that so eloquently with so clear and loud voice that everybody knew where it was coming from, everybody knew who was saying it. I found it a little disruptive and so I mustered up my courage and I went to her and I asked her the question of why do you say trespasses instead of debts because I thought maybe she had some Methodist in her background. But she didn't. She was born and bred Presbyterian, her father and her grandparents were all members of that church from way back. And she said, "let me tell you young man. "(O I long for the days somebody would call me young man.)She said, "my father , Mr. Murphy, was the banker in this town and Mr. Murphy believed that debts could never be forgiven, debts always had to be repaid so it would be highly irresponsible for anyone to pray forgive us our debts. "I never did change her mind but her father actually understood why we say debts and debtors in a way that maybe we don't always think about.

Trespasses doesn't have the strength of the word debts. You think of trespassing some place you think, O I just stepped on somebody's property; I better get off of their property and move along. But debts we understand. Debts we live with in our lives. Mortgages need to be paid, car loans need to be paid, credit card bills need to be paid. We understand debts. We understand the burden of debts. We understand the power that debts have over us. So when we pray forgive us our debts, we're making an acknowledgment that we have fallen far short of being the people that we were called to be. We've fallen far short of living our lives the way that God has called us to live them. We've fallen far short of being the people that God created us to be. We don't live the way, and we know this, we don't live the way that God wants us to live day in and day out. We fall far short of those goals that God has set for us. And so when we pray forgive us our debt we are acknowledging the need for God to be gracious to us, the need for God to forgive us, the need for God to wipe away that slate. And what Jesus was trying to help Peter to see, and for all of us to listen in on, was the fact that we live as people who say "forgive us our debts," we know that we owe God a debt that we could never ever repay. 10,000 denarii is nothing compared to what God has forgiven us in our lives. And so therefore if we live as forgiven people, if we live as people for whom our debts have been forgiven, then how ought we to live in our relationships with others? Forgive us our debts as we forgive our debtors. How are we doing with that? Are we keeping track? Are we maybe holding a grudge or two? Are we maybe remembering too painfully how someone has hurt us? Are we refusing to forgive anyone? As we have been forgiven, so we need to learn how to forgive. As we have been dealt with gracefully, we need to learn how to live gracefully. Not count against others what they have done wrong but to offer grace, forgiveness and love freely, openly and without any measurement, not seven times, not 77 times, not 70 times 7 times, freely, willingly, graciously offered and given. Forgive us our debts as we forgive our debtors. Would you pray with me?

Our heavenly Father we thank you that your grace abounds, that your mercy overflows, that you have welcomed us home as sons and daughters, not because of our worthiness but because of your graciousness. Help us O Lord to practice that grace in our lives. Teach us how to forgive as you have so freely forgiven us. We pray this in Jesus' name. Amen.

A Fair Wage
Matthew 20: 1-16

September 20, 2020

One of the rules of doing a worship service is to not have any dead time so what do is I walk up here and make you wait while I turn this on and plug this and all that good stuff. I apologize for that. This brief series that we been doing draws to a conclusion today. The series has been an attempt to help give us some tools for how to live in a difficult time of conflict that we seem to be in. An era where everyone is right and everyone is wrong and there's no middle ground. "Is you is or is you ain't" seems to be the question that is on everybody's tongue. But as Christians we are called to be a light into the world, to be salt that adds some flavor to the world. We are called to live a little bit differently. We cannot be a people who are divided or divisive in any way shape or form. We are called to be a people who work together and learn to love one another and live in that light and in that love as followers of Jesus Christ.

Our text today is an intriguing one. It's one that if you are doing a catalog of difficult sayings of Jesus or if you're going to write a book on challenging words that Jesus spoke, or one on confusing or perplexing words that Jesus spoke, this story, this parable that he taught, would be in that list. So let me just share it with all of you and see what we can learn in this passage that is so challenging for us. Yet it is one that I believe will help us to see and to understand a little bit better about how it is that we ought to live as Christians in a time of dissent. From the 20th chapter of Matthew beginning with the first verse. Jesus said this:

"For the kingdom of heaven is like a landowner who went out early in the morning to hire men to work in his vineyard. He agreed to pay them a denarius for the day and sent them into his vineyard. About the third hour he went out and saw others standing in the marketplace doing nothing. He told them, "You also go and work in my vineyard, and I will pay you whatever is right. ' So they

went. He went out again about the sixth hour and the ninth hour and did the same thing. About the eleventh hour he went out and found still others standing around. He asked them, 'Why have you been standing here all day long doing nothing?' 'Because no one has hired us,' they answered. He said to them, 'You also go and work in my vineyard.' When evening came, the owner of the vineyard said to his foreman, 'Call the workers and pay them their wages, beginning with the last ones hired and going on to the first. The workers who were hired about the eleventh hour came and each received a denarius. So when those came who were hired first, they expected to receive more. But each one of them also received a denarius. When they received it, they began to grumble against the landowner. 'These men who were hired last worked only one hour,' they said, 'and you have made them equal to us who have borne the burden of the work and the heat of the day.' But he answered one of them, 'Friend, I am not being unfair to you. Didn't you agree to work for a denarius? Take your pay and go. I want to give the man who was hired last the same as I gave you. Don't I have the right to do what I want with my own money? Or are you envious because I am generous? 'So the last will be first, and the first will be last.' 'May Lord bless this, a portion from his holy word.

We do live in a time where it seems to be that you either think this way or you think that way and if you think that way, you're wrong, or if you think this way, you're wrong, and we are in a very divisive, divided time and I think that this passage kind of speaks a little bit to that. Let me explain to you why I think that. Let me try to make some sense out of this passage for all of you. It is an interesting passage. It's a very intriguing passage and I had some fun with that as I was doing my preparation for this sermon today. I had some fun trying to see what other people might think about this passage. Let me give you just two examples of what I found as I did some research on this. The first that I found was a preacher who felt that this was a passage that proved that Jesus believed in everybody getting the same pay, that Jesus was one that felt that nobody should ever get paid more than anybody else. He went on to show that this passage showed that Jesus was a socialist and that was the way that we as Christians should live. That everybody, no matter what their education, their experience or their age, their training or their responsibilities - that everybody should be paid the same. That's what he got out of this passage. He saw Jesus as a young socialist helping us to see that the Christian way would be to follow that pattern.

I looked at a few others and then I found one that this person wanted to show that Jesus was a capitalist at heart. He looked at this and he said the very fact that the vineyard owner paid the last one more than he paid the first one on an hourly wage showed that some people bring more to the position and he went on to talk about how those who had been working all day were getting tired of the heat of the day, bringing in fresh ones because they were able to work harder and if they didn't get the crops in the money would've been lost and so therefore those who came later brought more value to the situation. Therefore, if you bring more value you ought to be paid a higher wage and this proved that Jesus was a capitalist at heart and if we are truly Christians we ought to be capitalists at heart.

Now you do that kind of research, you do that kind of listening to what others are saying and you just start to scratch your head. The problem with both of them is that we have this tendency. Let me teach you two new words. (I promised one of our members that I would teach a new word every week in the sermon) so today you're getting a two-fer. There are two words that I want you to learn. The first word is exegesis, the second word is eisegesis and don't ask me to spell either one of them. The word exegesis tells us that as we go to a text, as we go into the Scriptures that what we ought to do is try and mine them for the depth of the wisdom that is in there and you have to go with a blank slate - you have to go to that text and really get into it, listen to it, allow it to speak to you and to see what God is saying to you through that particular text. Eisegesis, the other word, is that human tendency we have to go to the text and see what it is that we want to see. We take ourselves and we put ourselves into that text. We read into the text our own presuppositions. I imagine that both of those preachers that I quoted were in essence doing eisegesis. They both went to the text to prove something that they already felt strongly about. The one felt strongly about socialism, the other felt strongly about capitalism and they looked at that text and of course what they saw was what they wanted to see.

Now the problem with eisegesis is it blinds us from seeing what we need to see. For this is a parable that the Jesus taught to those who were around him. There were all sorts of people that tagged along with Jesus. There were those who tried to follow him. Some were there to trip him up, some were there to learn from him, some were there just because he was a curiosity, but among those who were there with him were those who were deeply religious. There were those who were close to him, those disciples, those ones who were with him every step of the way and were trying to take it all in and there were those who were there who were Sadducees and Pharisees and others who were people of authority in the religious community of that time. They would come to listen and to watch what Jesus was doing and there is a little upset drawing because of the people that Jesus was dealing with. The Pharisees in particular didn't like the fact that Jesus was eating with sinners, spending his time with the hoi polloi, the unwanted, the unwashed, the unclean, the riffraff, you can call them whatever you want. He was not spending his time with the right people and they were not happy with that. They didn't see how he could call himself a man of God and spend his time with all the wrong people. They were not happy with that, they were not happy with the fact that he had included in his inner circle women and tax collectors and all sorts of people who would not quite make it in the religious world of that time. People who wouldn't make it as a Pharisee in particular but not any of the religious leadership would've accepted any of the people that Jesus was accepting and even the apostles themselves.

Those twelve who were closest to Jesus weren't always getting it right either. Later on we hear about James and John and their desire, one to sit on Jesus right hand one to sit on Jesus left hand and they were beginning to think that because they were disciples would have a higher position than others. Then Jesus tells this parable and they don't know what to do with it. He says the first shall be last in the last shall be first. Don't be upset if I'm generous, don't be upset if I'm generous. Don't be jealous, don't be angry, don't be upset if I'm generous.

You see Jesus was trying to help them to see that God's love is not limited. God's grace is freely given and that it doesn't matter whether you have lived your entire life as a saintly Christian person or whether you have come to faith in the last hours of your existence after living the most unholy life you could have lived, God still loves you. God's grace still abounds to you. He is trying to get his disciples, he is trying to get the Pharisees, he's trying to get anybody who would possibly listen to hear and to understand that none of us should ever be thinking of ourselves more highly than of others because we, by nature, do have the tendency. We do have the tendency to think "God can take really good care of me, I'm going to get a special place in heaven. I'm going to get one those big mansions. I'm not going to get some little condo on some side street in heaven. "But in God's eyes he sees us all the same as forgiven sinners whom he has loved deeply and dearly from the beginning. He wants us to understand that; he wants us to understand that when we deal with one another, we ought never to lord it over another, we ought never to think of ourselves more highly than anyone else. If God doesn't do a ranking, if God doesn't love someone more than he loves somebody else, than how is it that we can think of ourselves more highly than we think of others.

In this divisive age in which we live, one of the attributes of Jesus' life that we need to emulate the most is one of the most forgotten, humility. Humility - that's what this text is telling us. The first shall be last and last shall be first. God's turning everything upside down. If we have anything to brag about it's the knowledge that Jesus was willing to die for us but not for us alone. "For God so loved the world that he gave his one and only son. "We cannot think too highly of ourselves, we cannot think of ourselves as being better than anyone else, we cannot think of ourselves as having all of the answers - "if everybody would just listen to us this world would be a perfect place. " We need to humble ourselves, listen to one another, respect one another, see in the person who disagrees with us the heart of who it is that God loves in that person. This parable calls for us to do the hardest thing in a time such as this. It calls for us to walk humbly with our God. Jesus has turned things upside down. The world might have a pecking order, the world might say that this person is more valuable than that person but in God's eyes we are all equal, living as forgiven sinners by the grace of God's love. Would you pray with me?

Almighty and ever-loving God we would much prefer to go into your word and find the text that should prove us right but that's not why you gave your word to us. You gave your word to us to challenge us to confront our hearts, to change the way that we live, the way that we think, so that we can grow closer to becoming the people that you have called us to be. Humble us O Lord, as Jesus humbled himself upon the cross. Help us to live lives of humility so that we can see in others what it is that you see in them. We pray this in Jesus name had for his sake, Amen.

Nostalgia
Exodus 17: 1 - 7

September 27, 2020

Well done Praise Band, thank you. What a great song! When I get a text message on Saturday night saying, "We want to do this song right before the sermon. "I think, "there's a reason behind that and I'll find out what the reason is. "And it's obvious now because that was such a good song and leads us into our text for today. We're doing a series for five weeks and what we're doing is seeking to help people to find gratitude in our lives. Gratitude and thankfulness seem to be lost elements of how we live our lives right now. Maybe it's the situation, maybe it's the pandemic, maybe it's the election-year. Maybe it's all of everything that's happening, all at the same time, but we seem to be living in a time where we can't seem to recognize that which is good. We can't seem to find a way to just say "I appreciate this" or "I'm grateful for this" or "I'm thankful for this. "It's so much easier (and we all fall into the habit) we fall into the pattern of grousing and complaining and moping - you can list it all out. You know exactly what I'm talking about. So, we want to take a look and see what some of the barriers to gratitude might be for us. This week we're going to look at the first seven verses of the 17th chapter in the book of Exodus that goes right along with the song that was just shared with us this morning. So let's get the background on that song: the 17th chapter beginning with the first verse:

"The whole Israelite community set out from the Desert of Sin, traveling from place to place as the Lord, commanded. They camped at Rephidim, but there was no water for the people to drink. So they quarreled with Moses and said, "Give us water to drink. "Moses replied, "Why do you quarrel with me? Why do you put the Lord to the test? "But the people were thirsty for water there, and they grumbled against Moses. They said, "Why did you bring us up out of Egypt to make us and our children and livestock die of thirst? "Then Moses cried out to

the Lord, "What am I to do with these people? They are almost ready to stone me. "The Lord answered Moses, "Walk on ahead of the people. Take with you some of the elders of Israel and take in your hand the staff with which you struck the Nile and go. I will stand there before you by the rock at Horeb. Strike the rock, and water will come out of it for the people to drink. "So, Moses did this in the sight of the elders of Israel. And he called the place Massah and Meribah because the Israelites quarreled and because they tested the Lord saying, "Is the Lord among us or not? " May the Lord bless us a portion from his holy word.

These Israelites had a hard time seeing the big picture. They had a hard time remembering clearly and correctly. They were moaning and groaning to Moses making Moses' life miserable because they wanted to know why in the world did you drag us out here into the middle of nowhere to die? We were perfectly happy, we were perfectly content back in Egypt and you spoiled it all on us, taking us away from the comforts of our existence in Egypt. Now Moses had to be scratching his head at that one. That had to baffle him, that had to confuse him, that had to befuddle him and he was probably thinking to himself "what in the world are they remembering? What in the world is it that they want to go back to? Did they forget the hardships that they were enduring? Did they did they forget that they had to work long hard days? Did they forget that they were forced to make bricks but not given all of the materials that they needed to make the bricks? Did they forget that the Egyptians just went along and killed all of their firstborn? Did they forget that the life of slavery was the most horrendous existence that they could've imagined? Did they forget all the bad in all that they could remember was that they got the cot and three hots? Did they forget how God guided them - that one the Egyptians were close on their heels he spread open the waters so they could be free. Did they forget how God provided food for them? Did they forget all of the things that God had done for them to care for them and care about them and take care of them? "Moses had to be scratching his head. Then you and I read a passage like this - the story of the Israelites grumbling "I want to go back to Egypt! I want to go back to Egypt! " We start to scratch our heads asking, "What kind of people were they," not realizing that we're more like them than not. We let our recollections of the past prevent us from seeing what God is doing in the present.

I remember the summer before I started seminary, I was given the opportunity to preach at Langcliffe Presbyterian Church in Avoca Pennsylvania. (Nobody knows where that is - that's okay. It's where the airport is for Scranton - Wilkes-Barre but you don't need to know that.)I was given the opportunity to preach that summer. I think I was I was hired to preach 12 weeks there. On the first Sunday I was there I arrived early, I met with the clerk of session and she gave me this tour of this beautiful, magnificent building and it was a just a wonderful building. As we were going through this church every room that we went into she would say something along the lines of "I remember when" or "well we used to" or "I miss when we were. . . "She didn't pass a single room without harkening back to the glory days of Langcliffe Presbyterian Church, but not once in our conversation that day did she talk about anything that was happening there in the present. She was so caught up in what the church used to be that she could not see what God was doing in the current day. We do that. We do that all the time . . . (Wray didn't I start off (no, you don't have to run) Did you see him make for the door as soon as I called his name? What was the first thing I said you this morning? "I hate this. I miss having everybody here for church. I hate wearing this mask. I want it to go back to being the way it used to be. "Isn't that how I started the conversation this morning? Yes after the heart attack - he gave me a heart attack in the hallway because I did not know he was there and I walking along reading some papers in my hand and suddenly there's a human being in front of me. I didn't need my caffeine anymore after that.)But we do have that tendency to look backwards to be nostalgic and as we go back to the beauty of that song, the beauty of that song is that it's true that often times when we are looking backwards and longing for what used to be, we have a very different picture painted of what it actually was.

I remember one time not long after we arrived in Conklin and having left Wyalusing, I was lamenting to Debby how I missed Wyalusing and I start talking about how it was the perfect church and I never should've left there and I was going on and on about everything I missed about Wyalusing and she says to me, "Yeah, but you're forgetting. . . " and she started to tell me all the things that used to drive me crazy there and it is a wonderful church. I know there are some folks from Wyalusing watching but it is a wonderful church and I'm not saying it isn't. But we do have that tendency to paint a picture that is not fully accurate. We have the tendency to look back and forget the hardship, the negative, the difficulties.

I had a couple that I was visiting, and he was just lamenting longing for the good old days and everything and talking about prices and how expensive everything was and his wife finally said, "But what you forget dear, is that it didn't matter how expensive the bread was we still couldn't afford it then. We didn't have two nickels even if a loaf of bread was a nickel, we didn't have a nickel. You're forgetting that part. "

The Israelites looks back and painted a different picture than the reality that they were living in. We have that human tendency to look back and to think that everything was so much better than it is now. Worst part is we miss what God is doing in the here and now. We miss being grateful for what we have today, now in this hour, in this moment. I may not be a fan of social distancing, I may not be a fan of wearing the face mask, I may not be a fan of enduring all the things that we're enduring but let me just give this is as an example. This pandemic has helped us to be a better church. God is moving and working in the midst of this pandemic. We've been forced obviously into things such as, I was going to call it broadcasting but it's live streaming our services, then taping our services and making them available to people who just are not able to be here and that's a good thing. We're now doing something new and different that this pandemic forced us to do and this will become a part of who we are for years and years and years ahead, so that if somebody is shut in or somebody is not well or somebody is traveling, they can still be a part of the church they can still worship with us even though it would be remotely.

It has forced us to stay connected, this pandemic has forced us to think about how we take care of people and we have done such remarkable things to help people get through this pandemic, in little ways and in large ways. There has not been a person who has shared some difficulty with us that we have not been able to help them. We haven't turned down anyone who has said, "I'm in financial troubles."Because of your generosity, because of the church being forced to be the church, we have been helping so many people get through this circumstance that they find themselves into no fault of their own.

I can probably list out 20 or 30 more different ways that God is working and moving in our life together, but you can also see it in our own individual lives as well. How this situation has forced us to be more intentional about staying connected with one another, staying connected with family, staying connected with friends, of really causing us to recognize and value how important others are to us. This pandemic has caused us to not take for granted those things that matter the most to us: the people who make our lives wonderful. It's forced us to appreciate the opportunities that we have when we can be together or just to be in touch with somebody who is special to us. I could lament all day if you let me about all the things I miss about the way it used to be: two services, lots of people, hugs and handshakes and all sorts of things that are not a part of who we are and how were worshiping right now. But God still is working in our midst. God is still doing a good thing among us and within us. Let us not be like the children of Israel and spend our time complaining and lamenting for what used to be because it's not an accurate picture. but let us instead become a people who, even in the midst of times of trial and struggle, can see the presence of God working within us and working among us. Let us not lament, let us instead be grateful for what God is doing for us and with us and among us. Would you pray with me?

O God of grace and God of mercy forgive us for our tendency, our tendency to look back, to be nostalgic for a different time. Help us instead, O Lord, to keep our eyes focused upon you, upon your love, your grace, your mercy, your presence. Help us to be grateful for all that you're doing with us and among us. We pray this in Jesus name. Amen.

Worry
Philippians 4:1-9

October 4, 2020

We are doing this series of sermons; the series is entitled "Enemies of Gratitude" but you could just think about it as those things that seem to prevent us from being people who live lives that are fully grateful for all that God is doing for us in so many ways. There are so many things that pull us away from being able to appreciate and be grateful, to be thankful for so many things that are so good in this world. It seems to me that particularly right now in this time that we are living in and through, that our focus, intentionally or unintentionally, tends to be on the negative: upon those things that bring us down. One of those things that I think is probably the strongest barrier to us living lives of gratitude is that human tendency to worry. To worry about little things, to worry about big things, to worry about things that will happen, to worry about things that might happen and to worry about things that will never happen. That human tendency to worry about things draws us away from the ability to be grateful. I'd like to share with you a passage of scripture from the fourth chapter of Philippians, the first nine verses there. I have often said that the most difficult challenge of the Bible are Jesus' words to love your enemy. There are probably no more challenging words than that. But I have to say that this fourth chapter of Philippians might very well be a close second in terms of challenging us to live our lives in a way that is difficult at best. So let's hear what the apostle Paul is telling the church at Philippi and telling all of us as we overhear the words that he wrote to them so many years ago:

Therefore, my brothers, you whom I love and long for, my joy and crown, that is how you should stand firm in the Lord, dear friends!

I plead with Euodia and I plead with Syntyche to agree with each other in the Lord. Yes, and I ask you, loyal yokefellow, help these women who have contended at my side in the cause of the gospel, along with Clement and the rest of my fellow workers, whose names are in the book of life.

So far so good. Now it gets challenging. . . .

Rejoice in the Lord always. I will say it again, Rejoice! Let your gentleness be evident to all. The Lord is near. Do not be anxious about anything, but in everything, by prayer and petition, with thanksgiving, present your requests to God. And the peace of God, which transcends all understanding, will guard your hearts and your minds in Christ Jesus.

Finally, brothers and sisters, whatever is true, whatever is noble, whatever is right, whatever is pure, whatever is lovely, whatever is admirable - if anything is excellent or praiseworthy - think about such things. Whatever you have learned or received or heard from me, or seen in me - put it into practice. And the God of peace will be with you. May the Lord bless this a portion from his holy word.

Now I have to be honest with you, I think this series of sermons is literally and figuratively one of those series of sermons where the preacher points a finger out and at the same time is pointing three fingers back because I, like many of you, fall into the same traps, fall into the same situations where worry tends to take over. Now I have to be honest with you again because as I was working on this sermon and preparing this sermon, I all of a sudden realized my mind had wandered. I was not thinking about this passage of scripture from Philippians anymore. My mind had wandered and all of a sudden, I realized it and I caught myself worrying about a few different things. I start worrying about one and that brought up another to worry about and that brought up another to worry about and all of a sudden I realized I was sitting there at my desk getting absolutely anxious about things that, in retrospect, weren't worth getting anxious about in the first place. See that's the thing with worrying, 90% of the time you get all anxious and worried about things that aren't even going to happen, or you worry about something that is not nearly as bad as what your mind has made it out to be. But that, unfortunately, is our human nature.

How many times have you been with somebody, or you, yourself have been in that situation where tests are taken for a doctor and it's going to be two days or three days or a week before you get the results back from the doctor and where does your mind go? Your mind goes to the worst-case scenario. "This is going to be the death of me. I know I'm going to be dead in three weeks," and your mind just plays games with you and the worry and the anxiety and everything else take over. It's human nature.

The apostle Paul is trying to give us a different option - to look at life in a different way. I mean he starts off with that rejoice in the Lord always, again I say it rejoice no matter what situation you're in, rejoice, find the joy in it! But Paul, that isn't so easy. When things are falling down around you it's hard to rejoice. But he gives us that command but then it isn't until later that he gives us the means to fulfill that command.

The key is two things. Paul wants us to trust God. If we live in the knowledge of God's love and grace in each of our lives, if we live our lives in such a way, we know that God is going to work all things out for the good for those who love him, who are called according to his purpose. If we can keep that in our minds and if we could do that and transfer that worrying into prayer, then we'll be able to learn how to rejoice always in every situation good and bad. To take everything to the Lord with thanksgiving, to say to God, "you know what? I'm getting really worried about this but I'm going to trust you to take care of it."Then you can sigh a sigh of relief knowing that the God of love and mercy and grace is in control.

He also gives us another clue of how to live lives of gratitude and to diminish the worry that seems to overtake us. He tells us to not focus in on the negative. Instead, he tells us to focus in on the positive because it is so easy to see the negative, it's so easy to get caught up in everything that is bad, everything that is worrisome, everything that is troubling, that seems to be like six inches from our face. But even in the midst of bad, there is good. So, he says, "Whatever is true, whatever is noble, whatever is right, whatever is pure, whatever is lovely, whatever is admirable, if anything is excellent or praiseworthy, get them into your head. Think about those things. "

Worry can consume us. Worry can take over our lives. Worry can squeeze out any joy or happiness that we might have. But worry is not all that powerful, instead, turn to God, trust God, come to Him in prayer and thanksgiving, take those things that are troubling you and lay them at his feet and try and see and focus in on the positive.

My Presbyterian colleague, known to all as Mr. Rogers, once answered a child who was very anxious and told the child that no matter what situation you're in, look for the people who are doing good. So, no matter what situation we're in, no matter what the newspaper or the television or the radio or the social media might be telling us about everything and anything, look for the good because God is doing good in this world all the time. He has not left us, He has not abandoned us, He is still there with us and for us every step along the way. How can we really worry if God is in control and God loves us enough to have given of himself through his Son, Jesus Christ. Rejoice in the Lord always! Again, I'll say it, rejoice! Would you pray with me?

Our Heavenly Father, we do give you thanks for your goodness, for your presence in each of our lives. Forgive us when worry crowds out our ability to see your presence. Forgive us when worry crowds out our ability to see the good that you are doing. Forgive us when worry crowds out our ability to be grateful and thankful for all that you are and all that you are doing. We pray this in Jesus' name and for His sake, Amen.

Greed
Matthew 22: 15-22

October 18, 2020

When I was in 6th grade I made a plea to my mother. I said, "Mom, I don't want to go to church. I don't want to go to Sunday School. I don't want to do that anymore. "And I thought I had the perfect argument in place. I said, "I've already learned all the things in the Bible. I know every Bible story there is from the Old Testament to the New Testament. Why should I keep on going back? You're just going to start repeating yourselves. "You can tell I didn't win that argument. I still tend to go to church every Sunday. But we do sometimes have that mind set when we read a passage of scripture that we have heard before. We start out reading it and all of a sudden, our mind jumps to the end. We just start thinking "well I know what this one is, I know how it ends, I know how it works out, I know what it means, I'm just going through the motions of reading it again. "We have one of those passages that stands before us today. It's a very familiar story. You have probably heard it any number of times in church and Sunday School. It's been used on a number of occasions for Stewardship messages and other opportunities for it to be used, to be learned. But don't fall into the trap of thinking you know everything about it. Don't jump to the conclusion of where you think it's going to go. Instead, let's for these few moments transport ourselves back a couple thousand years ago and imagine all of us being the people who were gathered around Jesus that day when this incident took place. Let's go into it as if we're hearing it for the first time. Let's go into it hearing as if we are participants in this story. So, let's take a look in the Gospel according to Matthew in the 22nd chapter verses 15-22:

"Then the Pharisees went out and laid plans to trap him in his words. They sent their disciples to him along with the Herodians. "Teacher," they said, "we know

you are a man of integrity and that you teach the way of God in accordance with the truth. You aren't swayed by men, because you pay no attention to who they are. Tell us then, what is your opinion? Is it right to pay taxes to Caesar or not? 'But Jesus, knowing their evil intent, said, "You hypocrites, why are you trying to trap me? Show me the coin used for paying the tax. "They brought him a denarius and he asked them, "Whose portrait is this? And whose inscription? "'Caesar's," they replied. Then he said to them, "Give to Caesar what is Caesar's, and to God what is God's. "When they heard this, they were amazed. So they left him and went away. 'May the Lord bless this a portion from his holy word.

This is a familiar story. How many times have you heard it? Think back in your memory about how many times might you have heard this story and reflected upon this story and isn't it true, as you have heard this story, your first thought was, "Oh, this was one of the ones where Jesus tricks the people who were tricking him. "This is one of the ones that shows that Jesus is so much smarter than anybody around and they have tried to trip him up and he got them good. Isn't that kind of where you jump to with this? Isn't that where you land? That's not a bad place to land and I mean it is a simple truth and it is one that has been used by theologians to make some very important points. It has been used by theologians to point as a sign of the divinity of Jesus Christ: that his wisdom and his ability was far beyond any average human being would have. It's also been used by theologians who were trying to answer the question of whether or not the scriptures were written later by a bunch of disciples who wanted to make Jesus look better than he actually was. And the answer to that is, the bunch of disciples that we know weren't smart enough to come up with anything like this. So, there is a good reason, a good purpose to jumping to that conclusion but there's so much more here that we need to see, there's so much more that can help us to understand how it is that we ought to live our lives. How it is that lives filled with gratitude for who Christ is and what he has done for us ought to be lived out in real time and in all situations.

One of the things that jumped out at me, did you notice this? We're used to the Pharisees being the people who are trying to trip Jesus up or complaining what Jesus is doing. But did you notice in this incident, in this story out of Jesus' life there was a second group of people who were involved, the Herodians. It was the Pharisees and the Herodians conspiring together against Jesus. Now if you were a person standing in the crowd that day so many years ago, you would have been scratching your head unmercifully at the confusion of seeing those two groups working together. As a modern example, if you stepped up to today, that would be akin to the tea party and the democrat socialists working together to do something. I mean you had on one hand the Pharisees who could not stand the Roman government at all. It was an abomination to them that Rome was in control. It was an abomination to them that they weren't in control. It was an abomination to them that even the coinage that they used was a heresy because the coinage would have had the Emperor's face on it and would have had the statement that Caesar is a god. It would have been a proclamation of the divinity of Caesar: it would have been the title that was included on the coin there. And they were just appalled for being forced to use such horrendous things and to be part of such a way in their life. They wanted to have nothing to do with Rome, nothing to do with anything that was going on with Rome and they wanted to have them out and to be back in control again. But the Herodians on the other hand were Jewish people who took the tact of saying, "You know what? Let's make this work. Let's work together with them. Let's make the best out of this bad situation," so the Herodians became a part of the working of the Roman Empire and they would have had a vested interest in Jesus' answer. You know the Pharisees wanted Jesus to say no because it's a terrible thing to do; the Herodians wanted Jesus to say yes because they relied upon that income, that taxation was their livelihood and they needed that, wanted that. So, you had these two desperate parties working together to conspire against Jesus and Jesus recognized "there's something wrong when these two groups are working together. "And so, he picked up on that and he said oh I see what you're up to. I got it now. You are up to something here. So, he turns the tables on them.

Did you like how they approached Jesus? "You're the best thing since apple pie and ice cream, you're the most wonderful teacher we've ever had. You're never going to give us any bad answers. . . oh, by the way, it is lawful to pay taxes or not lawful to pay taxes? Should we support the Roman government, or should we be rebellious towards the Roman government? What should we do? "Schmooze him a little bit and then throw him the curve ball. That's pretty good. But Jesus recognized it through all their schmooze, through the curve ball question they threw at him. He turned it around to them and asked them the question. "Whose image is on this coin and whose title? "You know he's doing that as I've said before because the title was a proclamation of the divinity of Caesar and so he knew that would be appalling for them to say it out loud that it was Caesar's name, it was Caesar's image and Caesar's title that were on that coin. So, Jesus gives them the answer, "it's quite as simple as this: render unto Caesar what is Caesar's. It's his coin, you can give it back to him. And render unto God what is God's. "And we hear that, and we go yes! Good going Jesus you nailed them, you got them, you caught on to their trickery and you double-backed on them and you showed them that you could out-smart them and then we stop, and we go, render unto God what is God's. That's a lot harder than rendering unto Caesar what is Caesar's because everything is God's. Everything is God's, our lives, the air that we breathe, everything that we have, everything that we are belongs to God and so Jesus is telling us that our first and foremost responsibility is to place our lives in God's love and in God's control.

You know this translation and many translations use the word "give unto Caesar, give unto God" and I don't know if that's the best translation and I'll tell you why. I think that "render" is a better translation. I know that's an old English kind of word we don't use very much anymore. Have you "rendered" anything lately? I haven't used the word in a long time, but I'll tell you where I did use it. Back in Wyalusing, my first church, first town that I lived in fresh out of seminary. The main industry in that community was Taylor Packing. It was a meat packing plant, they slaughtered about 1,500 head a day and the president of Taylor Packing was Ken Taylor who was one of the members of Wyalusing Presbyterian Church and he offered me the opportunity to get a tour of the plant one day. I jumped at it and it was a fascinating tour - how mechanized everything is, how sanitary everything is and how methodical everything is but the one that interested me the most in the plant was what they called the rendering plant where they would take whatever was left over and make it into something useful. It could be dog food, cat food, it could be fertilizer to put back into the soil but nothing got wasted as Ken said they used everything but the "moo. "But that process of rendering, of making something useful, that's what Jesus is saying to us. To make our lives useful for God. To take everything that we are, everything that we have, everything that we do and use it for the Kingdom of God in the here and now. To make our lives useful - in terms of making this world more like God intended it to be. To take the words that we say, the conversations that we have and use them in a way that builds up the Kingdom instead of tearing it down and destroying it. To use our time in a way that builds up the Kingdom of God, that makes this world a better place, to live our lives and to use what we have in such a way when our lives are over and done on this earth that people say, "you know what? This world was a much better place for her presence here, a much better place for his being here. "It's about using all that we have and all that we are and the way that God intends it. To have our lives so focused in and on what God has done for us and what God wants us to do for him, that it changes our perspective, it changes the way that we live.

Remember those two groups, the Pharisees and the Herodians? They had chosen to put their trust and their faith in something other than God. The Pharisees put their trust, their faith and their system of rules and regulations and their ability to have power and their ability to be in control and to be the center of everything that was Jewish. The Herodians on the other hand put their faith, put their trust in the Roman empire and being able to work with them and work for them for their own good, for their own selfish purposes and we tend to do that as well in this divisive time in which we live. Living in this country that seems to be split right down the middle - democrat, republican, conservative, progressive, whatever the distinctions you might make, we can't put our trust in either, we can't put our hope and dreams there as well. If we are rendering unto God, then we must realize that the answers are not going to be found in whether this person is elected or that person is elected. It will not be the beginning of a new kingdom if this person is elected; it will not be the beginning of a new kingdom if that person is elected. It will not be the end of the world if this person is elected; it will not be the end of the world if that person is elected. God is still God and it is God whom we should always seek to serve and find in him our purpose, our meaning, our hope, our vision or how it is that we ought to live our lives. I wish, I wish that the better translation was "give unto God" because it would be merely a matter of writing a check. But the thought of rendering, of making our lives useful for the Kingdom of God demands a great deal more of us. Render unto Caesar what is Caesar's. Render unto God what is God's. Let us find our hope, purpose, our meaning and living in the one true God who loves us with an unfathomable love. Would you pray with me?

O God of grace and God of glory, you have called us to be your sons and daughters, to live our lives in your Kingdom, to follow your way, to do your will. Help us O Lord, as we seek to be useful to your Kingdom using our hopes, our dreams, our resources, our time, our energy to be the people of your Kingdom doing your work and your will to make this place a little bit more like the way you created it to be. We pray this all in Jesus' name, Amen.

Disappointment
Deuteronomy 34: 1-12

October 25, 2020

Today's sermon is drawing to a conclusion our series of sermons on those things that tend to be barriers for us, keeping us from living lives that are truly grateful. Those barriers that keep us from living lives that express not only gratitude and thankfulness but also find some peace and calmness in life. We've talked about a number of different ones over the past five Sundays now, but today's is probably the most pervasive one, the one that I think is the hardest to avoid and that is disappointment. Disappointment seems to be a very common aspect of human living. We have hopes and expectations, desires and dreams and in many occasions it seems sometimes as if the percentage is higher than we would ever want it to be; those hopes and dreams do not come to fruition and we end up being disappointed. Now sometimes we are greatly disappointed by things that in the long run really do not matter and trust me I know of which I speak on that topic. I am a New York Mets fan and a Penn State fan and both of them have disappointed me more times than I can count or even care to remember but in the long run it makes no difference whether they win or lose.

But in actuality there are those aspects of our lives that really do disappoint us, and we deal with that disappointment and it keeps us from living lives that are grateful in recognizing the blessings that we have. Let me share with you passage of Scripture (and I want to clarify what Darren said earlier. It's not that we don't trust you to listen to us. We do trust you listen to us but the Scriptures, for the most part, particularly the Old Testament were written as an after-the-fact kind of thing. Their original context was oral. The stories the histories would be passed from one generation to another generation. They would be memorized and then spoken into the next generation. They would memorize it and speak to the next generation. That was how much of what we now have as the Old

Testament was transmitted. And so there is a certain aspect of hearing the Scriptures that needs to be heard and if we just think of it as a written word, we're missing a powerful aspect of the Scriptures and that is the power of a story being told from one generation to another generation, from one person another person. So we really want you to get that experience to have that sense of hearing the story rather than having somebody reading something to you. I know it's a fairly minor distinction, but I think it's an important distinction for us to make.) So, let's listen now to the 34th chapter of Deuteronomy, the first 12 verses there and this is probably one of the most disappointing events in the pages of the Old Testament.

Then Moses climbed Mount Nebo from the plains of Moab to the top of Pisgah, across from Jericho. There the Lord showed him the whole land - from Gilead to Dan, all of Naphtali, the territory of Ephraim and Manasseh, all the land of Judah as far as the western sea, the Negev and the whole region from the Valley of Jericho, the City of Palms, as far as Zoar. Then the Lord said to him, "This is the land I promised on oath to Abraham, Isaac and Jacob when I said, 'I will give it to your descendants. I have let you see it with your eyes, but you will not cross' over into it. "And Moses, the servant of the Lord, died there in Moab, as the Lord had said. He buried him in Moab, in the valley opposite Beth Peor, but to this day no one knows where his grave is. Moses was 120 years old when he died, yet his eyes were not weak nor his strength gone. The Israelites grieved for Moses in the plains of Moab thirty days, until the time of weeping and mourning was over. Now Joshua son of Nun was filled with the spirit of wisdom because Moses had laid his hands on him. So the Israelites listened to him and did what the Lord had commanded Moses. Since then, no prophet has risen in Israel like Moses whom the Lord knew face to face, who did all those miraculous signs and wonders the Lord sent him to do in Egypt - to Pharoah and to all his officials and to his whole land. For no one has ever shown the mighty power or performed the awesome deeds that Moses did in the sight of all Israel. May Lord bless this a portion from his holy word.

Disappointment. Can you imagine being Moses? He did a job he never asked for. He tried to beg off of it. He didn't want to be one to lead the Israelites out of slavery. He never asked to be the one who would lead the Israelites through the wilderness. He never asked to be the one who would guide them, lead them, correct them, teach them. All those were aspects of what he did in those 40 years in the wilderness. He did a job that he never wanted, never sought, never desired in any way, shape, or form. He did a job that he thought would lead his people to a land flowing with milk and honey, a land more beautiful than they could ever imagine. He thought that he would be the one to lead them into the promised land where they could thrive and live and enjoy the goodness of life as a people following their God, doing his will, following his way in this world. That experience would make all the hard work worthwhile. Then Moses gets to Moab and God says, "Take a peek. There it is. Everything that I promised Abraham, Isaac, and Jacob. Everything I had promised you. Everything I promised the Israelites. It's all right there, right there before your eyes. As far as you can see in any given direction is the promised land and, oh, by the way, Moses this is as close as you get. " I would be very interested to know what Moses was thinking. I really would be interested, I know he wouldn't say anything out loud to God, there's no record of that, there's no stories ever told of him pleading with God to say, "You know, O come on, you didn't bring me this far to leave me here now did you? "But in his heart the thoughts must have been racing about how disappointing this would feel, to work that hard to experience everything that he experienced, to go through all the trials and tribulations, all the ups and downs, all of the things that happened along the way, all the good things, all the bad things, all of those with one goal in mind to get the people to the place God had promised. I don't know what other word you could use other than disappointment. He must have felt as low as low can be. Maybe in fact God's word to him caused him to die from a broken heart. We don't know what he died from because the story tells us that he was in good health. His eyesight was good, he was in good health, everything was working well, and he died at 120 years of age, so maybe it was disappointment that killed him. Maybe it was that he died from a broken heart. We can understand that, can't we? I think we've all been in situations where we had high hopes and expectations, we had dreams, we had things that we long for and then they all came crashing down. And we live for that disappointment.

But I don't know that Moses saw the whole story. I don't think he saw the big picture. I think that's part of what keeps us, when we are living with disappointment, from being able to be grateful, to be thankful because we are so caught up in the disappointment that we can't see what God is yet to do.

There's an old story, it's a gray dreary day I can tell you humorous story. There is an old story, an apocryphal story about a Presbyterian, an old-school Presbyterian. We'll call him Angus, that's a good Presbyterian name, good Scottish Presbyterian name and Angus was a faithful man who was very close to his God. One night he was praying to God and he said Lord I have served you faithfully throughout my life. I have tried to live my life in a manner that reflects who Jesus Christ is and who he wants us to be. I have served your church in every capacity possible willingly, joyfully, gladly and I've never asked you for anything in return Lord, but I like to ask you this one little favor if you would. He said, "Lord I would like to win the lottery. Would you do that for me Lord? I've been faithful to you, I'll continue to be faithful, I'll tithe my winnings, you don't have to worry about that" and then he hears this voice from heaven. The voice booms out and says, "Angus, I will grant your wish. You will win the lottery."So, Angus was delighted by that! He waited day in, day out, day in, day out, saying, "Lord, I haven't won the lottery yet. It's been weeks since you made me that promise, and I haven't won the lottery."Then the voice booms from heaven and says, "Angus, work with me here. At least buy a lottery ticket!" I know that's a silly story but sometimes when we are in the midst of our disappointment, sometimes when we are in the midst of dealing with difficult situations in our lives, we miss the bigger picture.

Moses' life was not summed up in that disappointment. As you hear the story being told, as the writer of Deuteronomy tells us about Moses' death, he doesn't stop with that. He talks about all the things that Moses accomplished with his life. Moses' life was not a disappointment to anyone. Moses life was one of faithfulness and goodness and accomplishment. Moses' life redeemed the people of Israel, brought them out of slavery and into the promised land. Moses and his disappointment did not have the chance to recognize and see the bigger picture and I think that's true for many of us as well. Often times as we live our lives, these disappointments come along. We get so focused on what we do not have, we get so focused in on what we have missed out on, we get so focused in on what we have lost that we miss what we still have. We become blinded to seeing what God is still doing in our hearts and in our lives. I know this is true because I think back upon the major disappointments of my life and I look at them now and I go why was I so worried about them? Why was I so devastated by them? I look back on them now and I see that what those disappointing times did was lead me into a different and better direction, a different and better situation. I'll give you a silly illustration. I had my heart broken a lot of times by women that I thought would be the person I would spend the rest my life with and I was sorely disappointed every time they dumped me like yesterday's newspaper (no, I'm not bitter.)But the fact is they prepared me for Debby and the wonderful life that I've had with her. Certainly, those were very disappointing days, disappointing times, disappointing situations but not a single one of them would have been the wonderful partner through life the Debby has been for me. You can get caught up in the disappointment or you can look to see how God is using that disappointment to lead you to a better place. If we get caught, if we get stuck in disappointment, it steals God's grace from us. It keeps us from living lives that are grateful and finding peace in God's presence in our hearts and in our lives. Disappointments are real, the pain is real and I'm not diminishing any of that but that is not a place we can dwell. We need to move through our disappointment to live our lives in the bigger picture of what God is doing in and through each one of us. Would you pray with me?

Almighty and ever-loving God how good you are to each and every one of us. You carry us, you lift us up, you get us through those times of disappointment in our lives. Oh heavenly father help us to not wallow in our disappointment but help us to live our lives in the sure and certain hope that we have through your love your grace, your providence, your mercy in each of our lives. Help us oh Lord when we cannot see the bigger picture to trust in you to be doing a good thing in and through us. We pray this in Jesus' name and for his sake. Amen.

The Other Side of the Curtain
Revelation 7: 9 - 17

November 1, 2020

We're beginning a new series of sermons this week. For four weeks Darren and I are going to talking with you about death. Your favorite topic, I know. It's something you long to talk about and you want us to be spending some time on it. But I do think it's good for us as Christians to deal with this because we live in a time where it seems as if we are trying to can get away from thinking seriously about what death is and what it means for us. And particularly as Christians I think we have lost our way in a very real sense because of the culture in which we live. We have gone to an extreme where we, in essence, are not taking death seriously. We will spend all sorts of time getting Halloween preparations ready and with the bones and all that sort of stuff. Debby will be the first one to tell you that I am the Halloween curmudgeon. It's not that I don't appreciate little children getting dressed up and handing out candy. I'm all in favor of handing out candy (one for you, one for me, one for you and one for me.) I'm okay with that, I'm very happy with that and I love little children and I love when they get to do pretend kinds of things and dress up to be something that they are not.

But what I have a hard time with is the dismissive way in which death is treated in this holiday. So many people decorate their yards and their houses with the most macabre sorts of decorations and maybe the fact is that I am a curmudgeon because I've experienced death too much. I lost track of the number funerals I've done. I have a record of them but I haven't counted them after I went over 300 funerals that I've done in the course of my 40 years of ministry. I have a hunch it is closer to 400 at this point in time and out of that number I would say more than half of them more than half of them were people that I knew. People I liked, people I enjoyed, people that I loved, people that I admired, people that I appreciated, people that to this day I still sorely miss. But we live in a time when death is not paid serious attention. We don't give it the credit that it needs to get. And now we're going to spend four weeks talking about that. Now just make it doubly uncomfortable, we're going to be reading a text from the book of Revelation which I know is 99% of people's not their favorite book of the Bible because it makes you very uncomfortable. You have questions and wonder about a lot of the symbolism and so on that goes on in the book of Revelation. But for today I want us look at the seventh chapter of Revelation beginning with the ninth verse:

"After this I looked and there before me was a great multitude that no one could count, from every nation, tribe, people and language, standing before the throne, and in front of the Lamb. They were wearing white robes and were holding palm branches in their hands. And they cried out in a loud voice: "Salvation belongs to our God, who sits on the throne, and to the Lamb. "All the angels were standing around the throne and around the elders and the four living creatures. They fell down on their faces before the throne and worshiped God, saying: Amen! Praise and glory and wisdom and thanks and honor and power and strength be to our God for ever and ever. Amen! Then one of the elders asked me, "These in white robes - who are they, and where did they come from? "I answered, "Sir, you know. "And he said, "These are they who have come out of the great tribulation; they have washed their robes and made them white in the blood of the Lamb. Therefore, "They are before the throne of God and serve him day and night in his temple, and he who sits on the throne will spread his tent over them. Never again will they hunger; never again will they thirst. The sun will not beat upon the, nor any scorching heat. For the Lamb at the center of the throne will be their shepherd; he will lead them to springs of living water. "And God will wipe away ever tear from their eyes. 'May the Lord bless this, a portion from his holy word.

Yes, it is a strange, strange time in which we find ourselves living culturally in terms of understanding what death is. We seem to either avoid it or demean it. For instance, over the course of my 40 years one of the things that I have noticed (now you can't count 2020 in any of these observations. 2020 is a world unto itself. We'll go back to 2019 and look forward to 2021) but in my observation fewer and fewer people are going to funeral services. Forty years ago, you might have a handful that would go to the calling hours but you would have a packed house for the funeral service. More recently it's vice a versa. You might have a packed house of people who will make their way quickly through the calling hours and then the day of the funeral itself, a good handful might be there. Nothing like what it was 40 years ago. We've grown discomforted by death and so we don't like to think about it, we don't want to spend any time dealing with it, so we go to the funeral home, we pay our respects, and we get out of there. We don't want to sit through a service, we don't hear anything about it, we don't want to experience it. We simply want to just go on with life as if death never happens.

We culturally demean death. I mean look at all the movies and other things that are out there now and I remember the word this time: zombies, the undead, and that whole thing. We just laugh at that and think, "Oh that's ridiculous and how funny that is. " What we are doing is demeaning death. We either dismiss it or we demean it. But the reality is death is a part of life. Death is a part of our existence and death is something that we as Christians need to have the ability to comprehend and understand, more fully, more clearly, more helpfully, more hopefully, what death means for each of us.

This passage of Scripture from the book of Revelation is one that I hope brings our hearts and minds some comfort, some hope, some perspective on death because in a very real sense this book of Revelation is a peeking through the curtain from this world into the next world, from this world into a glimpse, a small glimpse, a tiny glimpse of what the heavenly kingdom is all about. In this particular passage in the seventh chapter of Revelation we are told that the kingdom of heaven really knows no measure, it knows no constraint, it knows no barriers that we have in our world today because the first thing that the writer of Revelation tells us in his observation is that there are people from every tribe, every nation, every tongue, every language, they're all there and how many are they? How big is the kingdom of heaven? How open and receptive is the kingdom of heaven? We can't even count. You cannot count the number of people in the heavenly kingdom. God's love is so broad and so grand and so wide and so merciful that any of our human barriers any of our human distinctions that we make in this lifetime are washed away and there will be people in the heavenly kingdom from every corner of the world, every place, every time, every generation, every language, every color, every cultural group will be in the heavenly kingdom. It is that bold, that broad, that open to all people. It goes on to tell us that it is because of the Lamb, it is because of Jesus Christ and what he has done for us that that the kingdom of heaven is open to all peoples through his through his blood, through his sacrifice. Open to us because of the gift of his life, death, and resurrection. That place is a place where there's no sorrow or suffering. The writer of Revelation uses the imagery that they will hunger no more, they will thirst no more, the sun will not strike them, nor any scorching heat and the Lamb will guide them to springs of the water of life and he will wipe away every tear from their eyes. The blood of Christ will wash away all the ills, all the pain, all of the suffering, all of the sorrow of this life and we'll be living in a place that is more beautiful that you and I could ever perceive it to be.

I don't want you to be mistaken that death has lost its power because death is yet still a very powerful enemy to all of us. Death steals from us, death this takes from us those opportunities that we would have wanted to have had with those whom we have loved so dearly. Death takes away from us those people whom we have held so closely in our hearts and in our lives. Death still inflicts pain upon us. There's no getting around that. Dietrich Bonhoeffer wrote a wonderful piece in which he talks about the fact that death takes somebody away from us and when death takes that loved one away from us, there's a hole in our hearts. He says don't try to fill that hole with anything. Allow that hole to be there because it stands as a reminder of the one whom you have loved whom you're missing now, and you don't ever want to lose that memory from your lives.

So, pain is a part of death for us. It is something that takes its toll upon us. It hurts, it makes us feel lost and alone. It makes us feel sad and makes us feel a lot of things and that's okay because that is in essence the cost of what love is. To have lost somebody, to feel that sorrow, to feel that sadness, to carry that empty spot in your heart is the cost of love because the fact is it doesn't matter how old someone is because if it's somebody that you have love deeply and dearly, if they're a hundred and 10 years old you're still losing them too soon. That's the power of love.

What the writer of Revelation wants us to see is that all those sorrows will be washed away, all that sadness will be gone, there will never be another tear shed. All the tears of this lifetime will be wiped away and we will rejoice being in the presence of a God of love and mercy grace. It's good news. That's very good news. It doesn't exempt us from the pain, doesn't exempt us from the sorrow but what it does is in the midst of that sorrow in the midst of that pain it inserts hope. Hope for that day for a grand reunion with all those who we have love so dearly who have gone before us. And that's good news.

In a few moments you and I will be celebrating the Lord's Supper together. It was given to us as a reminder, a very tangible reminder that we are united together. That's where the word communion comes from, being in common with each other, holding each other together and it's not just within a church, within a congregation, within a community, within a country, even within a generation of this world. It is a reminder that we hold one another in common, all of the saints who have gone before us, and that's why so important for us to have All Saints Day to be reminded of those who have touched our lives and helped us to understand the grace and love of Jesus Christ. It holds us in common with all those who have gone before us. It holds us in common with those who are yet to come, those whose lives we are touching today who will touch lives generations after you and I are in the heavenly kingdom. It is a reminder that while death is a very powerful enemy it's not the final victor! In Jesus Christ victory is ours. The power of death is very strong but it's not the final word. That's good news that in Jesus Christ, through the blood of the Lamb, there we're reminded of in this sacrament all of our sins will be washed away, all of our tears will be wiped away. Now that is good news. Would you pray with me?

Our loving heavenly father how can we ever thank you for the gift of your love in Jesus Christ. The gift that brings hope a gift that brings perspective the gifts that has conquered the power of death over each of our lives. We thank you Lord. Fill our hearts with that hope. In Jesus' name Amen.

Grieving with Hope
I Thessalonians 4: 13-18

November 8, 2020

We continue in our four weeks series of sermons that are dealing with the issue of death and it's an attempt on our part to help us to be informed and that's a key word in the passage we're going to read and think about today. It's important for us as Christians to have an understanding of how we can deal with one of life's inevitable features. And so, I'd like us to look today in a book that I have a hard time pronouncing so if I don't get through it you'll know which book I'm talking about. There's like six words that I can't pronounce and this is one of them. I was preaching in little Sugar Run Church when I was just starting out in ministry and the harder I tried to say the name of this book the less able I was to do it and it kept getting worse and worse with every attempt to say it. So, let me try it, so bear with me. 1st Thessalonians chapter 4 verses 13-18.

Brothers, we do not want you to be ignorant about those who fall asleep, or to grieve like the rest of men and women, who have no hope. We believe that Jesus died and rose again and so we believe that God will bring with Jesus those who have fallen asleep in him. According to the Lord's own word, we tell you that we who are still alive, who are left till the coming of the Lord, will certainly not precede those who have fallen asleep. For the Lord himself will come down from heaven, with a loud command with the voice of the archangel and with the trumpet call of God, and the dead in Christ will rise first. After that, we who are still alive and are left will be caught up together with them in the clouds to meet the Lord in the air. And so we will be with the Lord forever. Therefore encourage each other with these words. May the Lord bless this a portion from his Holy Word.

We don't know for sure what was going on in the church in Thessalonica (I practiced that one long and hard too) when Paul was writing to them, but Paul had this concern that the church there in that city was having some questions as to what happens with those who die, particularly those who die before Jesus returns. We don't know exactly what their concerns were, we don't know exactly what it was they were worried about but we can see what Paul's answer is and so we get some little clues there as to what the questions or concerns might have been. Paul uses his words carefully here because he says he doesn't want them to be ignorant or uninformed. He wants them to know and to understand more clearly what is happening. He uses an interesting phrase, "I don't know" whether you picked up on this or not, but he uses an interesting phrase for those who have died. It's not a euphemism, we use all sorts of euphemisms to say somebody passed away, somebody's gone home, we use all these wonderful euphemisms that kind of soften the blow of somebody dying. But Paul is not using a euphemism here, he's using a descriptor. He says "those who have fallen asleep."Now why is that a descriptor and not a euphemism? It's a descriptor because Paul is trying to get them to see that the death that they experience is not a permanent thing. It's a temporary thing.

When we go to bed at night and we have the luxury of falling asleep and we rest and then the alarm goes off and we go "Whoa! Is it already time to get up?" If I reset your alarm and it went off at 2:00 a. m. and you thought it was 7:00 a. m. you wouldn't know the difference. That's how it is with sleep, it is outside the realm of time. And so, Paul is trying to help them to see that when somebody dies they are outside the realm of time, that they are in a temporary state and that they will wake up from that sleep, they will rise from being dead. And he's very clear about that because he wants us to have hope that as Jesus was dead and buried, he rose from the grave and he lives. He wants us to see that comparison that as Jesus was dead and is now alive so too those who are dead will yet be alive. He wants us to see that. He wants us to understand how death works and that it is just a temporary affliction before a permanent goodness. A temporary affliction before a permanent goodness. He wants us to see that so we can understand and have hope that as we face death, either the death of somebody we know and love or as we face our own death, that we face it not with fear but with hope.

Now, he goes on to say he doesn't want us to grieve like those who have no hope. That's important for us to see because he's trying to make a distinction there for us in this letter to the church. He's trying to help us to see that it is not that we who have hope, we who understand death ought not to grieve. He's not saying to us that it's bad for a Christian to cry or it's bad for a Christian to be saddened or it's bad for a Christian to have that empty spot in their heart for somebody they have loved and have lost. He says it's okay to grieve but we ought not to grieve like those who have no hope. He's making that distinction for us.

A good number of years ago when I was in my first church, the fellow that had the funeral home next door to the church, a young man by the name of John McHenry, called me up and he said, "Steve, I have a family here and they really, really need a pastor. "And I said, "John, they don't have a pastor that anybody in the family is related to? "And he said, "No, not anybody in this family has ever gone church. Would you come and do the service for their mom? "I said, "Sure, I'll do that for you John. "So, I went, met with the family a little bit, admittedly it was a little awkward. They didn't know what to do with me so they were a little uncomfortable. I was probably one of the first pastors they ever talked one-on-one with and as I was doing the service, I was struck, I was absolutely struck by the way that they were grieving. I was absolutely struck by the wailing and the weeping and the mourning that was taking place. I had never ever experienced anything like that before because they were grieving in a way that said there is no hope. They were grieving in a way that said they would never see their mother again. They were grieving in a grief that all was lost, never to be redeemed, never to be found again.

Paul wants us to see that as Christians it's okay to grieve but don't grieve without hope. We grieve with the hope that we will be reunited again with those whom we have loved who have gone before us. And he's pretty clear about that because he speaks about Christ's coming and the dead in Christ will be raised first and at his coming those who are alive at the time will join together and we'll all be in that heavenly kingdom, in a place of peace and joy and comfort.

But there's another element to this that gets lost in most readings of this passage and it's that 18th verse where he says remember these things and encourage each other with these words. *Encourage each other with these words.* You see he is trying to tell us that we as the church grieve together and we encourage each other together. That sometimes when somebody loses someone very dear to their heart, that their faith might waiver, their pain might be overtaking them: that when their own faith isn't able to carry them through that hour, that we as the church, we as the body of Christ together, need to be there with and for each other and to pick up that person who is grieving and carry them with the hope that we have in our hearts until they have the strength and the ability to have that hope themselves.

That's been one of the side problems with this COVID-19. One of the unanticipated issues with the spatial separation and the lockdowns and etc. that I don't think anybody thought about was the fact that we have greatly diminished the church's ability to be the church for those who grieve. We've had, I think, three of our members pass away this year whose funerals have been put off until some other time and that's hard. The others have had very small services with just a hand full of people there and that's hard too because one of the reasons that we have funerals, one of the reasons that we do memorial services, one of the reasons that we do the little luncheons afterward is to be that encouraging body, to be those people who lift up those who are in distress, lift up those who are in periods of mourning and this COVID-19 has stolen away from us that ability to be the church and to serve others with love and grace in the hours where they so desperately need that love and that grace.

"Therefore encourage each other with these words" the apostle Paul says. In other words, don't be afraid to talk about death. Use the right words when you do and sometimes just simply listen and show compassion and care. I've often said that one of the interesting books that I could write would be the dumbest things ever said in a funeral home but there are so many good things that we should say to encourage, to uplift, to help out people who are going through those challenging times. The words of hope, the words of encouragement that death is just a temporary affliction before a greater good. The apostle Paul didn't want us to be ignorant, didn't want us to be uninformed. He wanted us to know and to understand that death has been conquered and that it's okay to grieve; it's still painful, it's still hurtful but don't grieve without hope and encourage each other with those words of hope and love and mercy that come from God through his love for us. Would you pray with me?

Almighty and ever-loving heavenly Father, we thank you for the hope that you have given to us in your son Jesus Christ whose life, whose death, whose resurrection gives us the ultimate hope that when everything is said and done it is you who will have said it and you who will have done it and that you will carry us home to the heavenly kingdom where every tear is wiped away. We give you thanks, O Lord, for your Son Jesus Christ in whose name we pray, Amen.

How Many Shopping Days Left?
Psalm 90: 1-12

November 15, 2020

That was beautiful. Thank you. Just beautiful. You go from such a beautiful moment and now I'm going to talk about death. I don't think I'm the brightest bulb in the pack. We're going to look today at the 90th Psalm. It's not like the 23rd Psalm, it's not like the 150th Psalm, it's not like a lot of other Psalms but it is one that does give us a glimpse into something that maybe we don't want to think about but maybe we ought to think about little bit more and that is how are our days numbered. Kind of a cute title to the sermon is "How Many Shopping Days Left?" But it is a question of how are our days numbered and that and that incurs upon it a secondary question which may be ought to be the primary question is how is it that we live our lives? We use the 90th Psalm is our Psalter reading earlier so let me just pick a few verses here. I want to do verses 9 and 10 and then skip down to verse 12.

*"For all our days pass away under your wrath; our years come to an end like a sigh. The days of our life are seventy years or perhaps eighty if we are strong. Even then their span is but toil and trouble, they are soon gone and we fly away. So teach us to count our days that we may gain a wise heart. "*May the Lord bless this a portion from his holy word.

I will grant you that the 90th Psalm and this portion of it are probably not the verses that you're going to want to run home and calligraphy or to do counted cross stitch and hang it on the wall of your living room. But I think it nonetheless raises some good questions that we need to think about with our lives and I know Darren and I have, well Darren gets to torture you next week, but I've tortured you these past three weeks on the topic of death. But the previous two weeks have been more about how we deal with death and generality and how do we deal with the grief and pain and anxiety of the death of somebody or some people that we love. Now this week I've gone from preaching to meddling because we need to think about our own lives - how it is that we that we look at the specter of death in each of our lives personally. And I've got a birthday coming up this week, it's one of those milestone birthdays I'll be honest about that, but it also reminds me of the fact that given what heredity is, I know Debby is not going to want me to tell you this part, but looking back at four generations of Starzer men, none of us have ever made it past 76. My great-great-grandfather, my great-grandfather, my grandfather, my father and in each generation, there were three brothers and none of the three brothers have ever made it past 76. Matter of fact we lost a year with my dad's generation. It's now 75. I do have to tell you this - that I do have my oldest brother, we did lose my brother John at 59, but my oldest brother Paul is 73 this year and boy am I praying for him. I am behind him 110% all the way to break this life span issue that the Starzer men seem to have and actually it's (Debby close your ears) it's even worse for the Starzer women, the wives. My great-grandfather is an example was widowed twice before he is 29 years of age. So, it's must be really rough to be married to Starzer men and you must have really tremendous stamina so I'm really proud of you Debby. Hang in there, you're doing great. But I do look at that and you can't help but think about it you go okay that gives me 10-11 maybe 11-1/2 good years left, and it makes you wonder. What is it that the psalmist is trying say? Is the psalmist trying to say, "you know woe is me, I'm going to live long a little while and then I'm going to die?" Or is the psalmist trying to say that we need to consider the fragility of life - that all of us are given just so many years and then the question comes, what is it that we do with those years that we are given? The 12th verse says so teach us to count our days so that we may gain a wise heart. In other words, help us to recognize the brevity of life so that we have the wisdom to use every day, every year, every moment that we have fulfilling God's call upon each of our lives. To use the gifts that God has given to us with our lives, to use that gift of each day of our lives in a way that reflects God's love for us.

A good number of years ago now I received one of those phone calls that pastors do not like to get. It was a call from a family member of one of the older couples in the church and she said you need to know that dad got word from his doctor that there is nothing more that they can do for him. The cancer was going to win. She said would you stop over see them? I said, "surely I will. " Now Freeman and Margaret Brooks are two of the most incredible people I've ever met my life. She was a retired schoolteacher, and he was a retired mechanic for a local bakery. He kept the trucks going so the baked goods could get out. Just incredible people. The kind of people that you immediately love and respect and admire so you can imagine how I how I felt that day by realizing I had to make that drive to their house and I had to come up with some words to say as their pastor to be comforting and encouraging and to help give them some strength to face this which life was bringing upon them. It was only about a mile from the church to their house but as I recall it was the longest mile I ever drove. As I recall I did not get any speeding tickets in that mile and when I got to the house got out of the car, I don't think I could've taken smaller steps going up to that front door, but I made it. I rang the doorbell, and I didn't know what I was going to say, I didn't know how I was going to reacted, and I didn't know how I was going to handle that situation and Mrs. Brooks met me at the door and welcomed me in the big smile and she says I'm glad you're here. Come on in, let's visit. Freeman was in the living room to the right sitting on a bed that they had set up for him in there and Margaret sat down next to him and I'm still trying to conjure up in my mind what words might I offer, what comfort might I say, what scripture passages might I quote, what should I be doing as your pastor and I go into that room and I see Freeman sitting there and he smiles at me. He said, "I'm glad to see you. I want you to know that I'm okay with this. The Lord promised me three score and 10 years. Since I've had 12 bonus years, I have nothing to complain about. "And then we spent the next hour just listening to him recount all the blessings in his life all of the people that touched his life. He talked about all the blessings that his family had given to him, all the joys of his 60+ years of marriage and all of the happiness that his kids brought, the grandkids and so on and people that he knew, good friends that he had, friends that he worked with, friends from the community and his church and how much his church is meant to him and how glad he was to be able to serve as an elder and to be able to teach a Sunday school class and to be able to fix things around the church and how glad he was to be able to do all those things and how grateful he was the God gave them 82 years to do his work in this world. Now that my friends is counting your days and having a wise heart. For none of us know how many days we have. I mean I can extrapolate out on the heredity thing, but I really am counting on my brother Paul to break that cycle for us, But none of us know. So, the goal the challenge for us to have a wise heart is to try to make the most out of every day that we have, to count every day as a blessing to count every day as an opportunity to do God's work God's will in this world, to love your neighbor as yourself, to love the Lord your God with heart and strength in mind and soul, to walk humbly with your God. to love mercy and to practice justice, to live each day as an opportunity to be God's people in this world. to be ambassadors of God's love to those who are around you, to friends, family members, strangers, whoever God puts into your life to share with them through the way that you live your life. God's love, grace, mercy, to make the most out of every day that we are given whether we have one more day or a thousand more days or who knows how many days. No matter how many days are counted out before us to use each one of them to be God's people in this world.

One more week were done with this topic but sometimes you just have to think about our own lives because if we don't think about the limits in our lives, we might miss out on the opportunities that we otherwise would put off to some other day, I'll start that next year or the year after. Count each day as a blessing. Count each day as a gift from God filled with opportunities to do God's work in this world and there's no limit to that. There is a woman by the name of Evelyn weeks who is a pillar of the church that I was serving, and Evelyn was in the final days, weeks of her life and she was talking with me and she said Steve I hate the fact that I can't do the things I used to do. She used to run a clothing closet to help people out with the clothes, winter jackets, whatever they might need she had her whole basement was filled with clothes for other people that she gave out anybody who needed that. She would help with baking food for anybody at any time. I could go on with a list of all the things that Evelyn did for the community and for the church and she was lamenting the fact that she didn't have the ability to do all those things that were so important to her in her life and she was regretting that she was lying there in that bed saying she couldn't do Christ's work anymore. I said to her, "Evelyn one of the things you do best is you pray with your whole heart. You can't do the baking, you can't do the closing closet but I really need you to keep praying. "So, I made her a deal. I would bring her a list and she would go through that list and pray for everyone. That's the wisdom of the heart, to use each day no matter what situation we may be in, to use each day doing God's work, doing God's will in this world, practicing what he is called us to be as we live out each day that he gives to us as a blessing, as a present. Would you pray with me?

Almighty and ever-loving God, we thank you for each day of our lives for each day brings with it opportunities to be your people, to live our lives as your sons and daughters, to do your work and your will in this world. Help us oh Lord to have wise hearts recognizing and knowing that there's always more for us to do for your kingdom in the here and now. We pray this in Jesus name. Amen.

The End of the World as We Know It
Mark 13: 24-37

November 29, 2020

Darren and I were talking in the hallway just before we came in and I said to Darren, "It's kind of a tough sermon today. I hope I can do it again after the early service" and he says to me with those wonderful words of encouragement that a colleague and friend can offer, he says, "Don't worry, Jerry is singing today. Nobody is going to remember anything you said. "So, thank you Jerry, you made my day.

We have jumped into Advent. Somebody asked me earlier today how does this all work? Well, it is the four Sundays prior to Christmas that make up the season of Advent. Sometimes there's a Sunday in between Thanksgiving and the start of Advent but I think maybe three out of every four it actually jumps directly from Thanksgiving into Advent. On top of that that confusion is the fact that we as the Christian church seem to be marching against the stream of the world, because no matter where you go, it's already Christmas. If you go into a store or turn on a radio, no matter where you look the decorations are all up at people's houses. You drive through your neighborhood and houses are beautifully decorated for Christmas. But yet I stand in front of you and say Christmas is not until December 25. We are in the season of Advent and on the Christian calendar this is the beginning for us. I mean, it would not be out of line for me in the Christian calendar to say happy new year everyone because this is the beginning of our Christian year. This is the beginning of our seeking to fully understand the person and work of Jesus Christ and what that means for us in so many ways. So, we stand in this kind of juxtaposition, this clashing between the world around us which is ready to celebrate Christmas. (If you buy it early enough, they will even celebrate it sooner.)But to celebrate Christmas starting with the day of Thanksgiving which leads directly into Christmas: we're saying wait! Hold up! There's preparation the needs to be done. There is work that must be done in order for us to arrive at Christmas day. So it is that we have this wonderful season of Advent. A time for us to get ready, to prepare, to make ourselves ready for Christmas day.

If ever there was a time, as Darren alluded in his prayer, if ever there was a time where we need Advent: Advent being a season of hope and expectation, now is one of those times. We live in a time of unprecedented disruption. Nothing is as it has been, nothing is as it should be, nothing is the way that we wanted to be. We live in a time where we join with the early church with the phrase Maranatha: even so come quickly. Whereas the early church was saying it to welcome Jesus' return, we are in a time where we are ready to say "Maranatha: even so come quickly vaccination. "Here's my shoulder let's get at it. It's a time of disruption, it's a time when everything is out of kilter. I mean who ever imagined that I would ever be preaching to a bunch of people with face masks on? It kind of has an old west feel to it and I'm ready to raise my hands and say here's my wallet just take it. In the early church it was a time of disruption and confusion and things weren't as they should be or ought to be. It just was one of those eras when nothing was quite right and so there was this eager expectation for the coming of the day when all the wrongs would be made right.

So, let's take a look at this passage of Scripture that we have in the gospel according to Mark in the 13th chapter beginning with the 24th verse. We'll read verses 24 to the end of the chapter.

"But in those days after that suffering, 'the sun will be darkened, and the moon will not give its light; the stars will be falling from heaven, and the powers in the heavens will be shaken.' Then they will see the Son of Man coming in clouds the great power and glory. Then he will send out the angels and gather his elect from the four winds, from the ends of the earth to the ends of heavens. From the fig tree learn its lesson. As soon as its branch becomes tender and puts forth its leaves you know that summer is near. So also when you see these things taking place, you know that he is near at the very gates. Truly I tell you this generation will not pass away until all these things have taken place. Heaven and earth will pass away but my words will not pass away. But about that day or hour no one knows,

neither the angels in heaven nor the Son but only the Father. Beware! Keep alert! For you do not know when the time will come. It is like a man going on a journey when he leaves home and puts his slaves in charge each with his work and commands the doorkeeper to be on watch. Therefore keep awake. For you do not know when the master of the house will come -in the evening, or at midnight, or at the cock crow, or at dawn or else he may find you asleep when he comes suddenly. What I say to you, I say to all keep awake! May the Lord bless us a portion from his Holy Word.

Now I've said this many times before. Mark is my favorite gospel. I like the Gospel of Mark because Mark is succinct, straightforward, right to the point, he is one who just keeps you moving along. While Mark is grammatically probably the worst of the four Gospels, Mark is nonetheless, I think, the best written of the four Gospels because of that sense of urgency in the way that Mark has of drawing us into the gospel story, bringing us in there and making us a part of it and making it our responsibility to do something with the story that he's telling. Mark doesn't include everything in his gospel that Matthew and Luke do and certainly not what John includes as well. Mark is the shortest of the four Gospels. It is the briefest telling of the good news of Jesus Christ. So, you get to a passage like this and it's not what you expect in Mark's gospel. You would think that Mark with his sense of urgency and his sense of succinctness of just clarifying and distilling down what Jesus is saying and doing, that he would've left this one for another gospel writer maybe somebody else to tell. How does this fit in and why in the world did Mark ever include this passage this story out of Jesus teaching. Why in the world that Mark include that? But he did and we have to take a look at it and we have to seek to understand what it is that Mark is trying to get across to us.

You see Mark was trying to help us to see that maybe not his term but our term in the Christian church is that this season of Advent, the season of expectation, is a two-pronged expectation. It is, on the one hand, a season of us preparing our hearts and getting our minds ready to fully comprehend and to fully take into ourselves the good news of the birth of the Babe of Bethlehem. Advent allows us that opportunity to see and to understand more fully and more completely why it is that we so wonderfully celebrate the birth of Babe of Bethlehem. Why it is so important for us to know and to understand meaning of "the word become flesh and dwell among us. "Advent gives us that opportunity to build up to Christmas day so that we fully comprehend, and we fully take upon ourselves what it means that God loves us enough to take upon Himself, through his son Jesus Christ, human form to be among us to teach us, to show us how it is that we ought to live. So, Advent has that one primary role that we often times look at and we try to use that season as best as we can. We try to do extra things during the season of Advent. That's why we're making sure that everybody has an Advent devotional to take home with you just to do a little extra work in this season of preparation in this season of expectation and hope as we get our hearts and our minds ready for the birth of babe of Bethlehem.

But from the earliest church on, Advent also had a second purpose tacked onto it and that tact was the recognition that Christ shall come again. Maranatha even so come quickly Lord Jesus. That expectation that the Christ shall return and bring everything to fruition, that all the wrongs will be made right, all the tears will be wiped away, all the sorrow will be diminished. You see Advent is that two-pronged approach: the expectation of the birth of the Babe of Bethlehem but then the recognition that Christ's person and work that began in that birth in Bethlehem so many years ago, those 33 years that he had among us were just a down payment of what is yet to come. That Jesus gave us the down payment, the earnest payment, on what God would someday fulfill in completeness and entirety. Therefore, we live in this season of Advent preparing ourselves and reminding ourselves, preparing for the birth of the Babe of Bethlehem and reminding ourselves that that same person shall return one day.

Mark wants us to be sure we understand that the Christ's return could come at any time. He does quote Jesus saying that only the Father knows, none of us can know the day or the time or the place. It's not for us to know. Jesus himself did not know. It is for God alone to know when all of time will come together in that fruition of what Christ began with his life and work and ministry. But Mark wants us to see as well because Mark is the practical gospel. He wants us to see that this eager expectation is not a kick up your feet, sit back and wait for Jesus to come but it is instead for us to be alert, to be awake, to be active, to be God's people in the here and now. We are called to live our lives in such a way that if Christ were to return on this day, on this hour, that our lives would prove to be ready for his return. In other words Mark wants us to see that what Christ has begun in his life and ministry, the way that he lived his life in selfless love, such selfless love that even took him to the cross, such selfless love that he would die for us, is the example of how we ought to be living our lives in this "in between" time. . . not sitting back with our easy chairs and waiting for his return but living our lives in an active way where we exemplify what that kingdom is going to look like. We ought to be working for the kingdom in the here and now. When he says that we ought to be alert, keep awake, that's exactly what he's telling us to do, to be doing what we are called to do to live our lives in a manner that reflects Jesus Christ working in and through us: to live our lives not in the expectation that we can sit back and wait for God to do everything but that we are so anxious to get to that point that we are willing to work towards that end.

So, Advent is a season of preparation. Certainly, the preparation of our hearts and minds to fully hear and comprehend and to absorbed the good news of Jesus' birth but it is also time of preparation for the reality the Christ shall return and that we have work to do in the in-between time. Our preparation is living our lives in such a manner the Christ's love is reflected in and through us. That's being ready for Christ's return. Maranatha even so come quickly Lord Jesus. Would you pray with me?

Almighty and ever-loving God how we thank you for the gift of your son Jesus Christ, in his scant few years on this earth, we recognize a down payment for what is yet to come. Help us O Lord to live in eager expectation of Christ's presence in this world, to be reminded of his birth so many years ago and to be reminded that he is yet to come again. Help us to be ready Lord by doing your work and your will in this world. In Jesus name we pray, Amen.

Where the Wild Things Are
Isaiah 40: 1-11

December 6, 2020

Here we are in the second Sunday of the season of Advent. As we make this progression through the weeks of Advent, we do so in a manner that helps us to be mentally and spiritually and prayerfully prepared to receive the good news of the birth of the Babe of Bethlehem: to celebrate the Advent that has been - the coming of the Christ child - and to celebrate the Advent that shall be - His return someday. And so we like to look back in order to look forward and one of the ways we do that is by taking a look at some of the passages of scripture. We'll be doing that the next three Sundays as we are going to be studying passages of scripture from the pages of the Old Testament, the foundation that helps us build our preparation for the good news of the coming of Jesus Christ, his birth and his return.

So today I'd like us to look at a passage that is very much a part of our Advent traditions: that is the 40th chapter of Isaiah verses 1 - 11:

"Comfort, comfort my people, says your God. Speak tenderly to Jerusalem, and proclaim to her that her hard service has been completed, that her sin has been paid for that she has received from the Lord's hand double for all her sins. A voice of one calling: "In the desert prepare the way for the Lord; make straight in the wilderness a highway for our God. Every valley shall be raised up, every mountain and hill be made low; the rough ground shall become level, the rugged places a plain. And the glory of the Lord will be revealed, and all mankind together will see it. For the mouth of the Lord has spoken. "A voice says, "cry out. "And I said, "What shall I cry? ""All men are like grass, and all their glory is like the flowers of the field. The grass withers and the flowers fall, because the breath of the Lord blows on them. Surely the people are grass. The grass withers and the flowers fall, but the word of our God stands forever. "You who bring good tidings to Zion, go up on a high mountain. You who bring good tidings to Jerusalem, lift up your voice with a shout, lift it up, do not be afraid: say to

the towns of Judah, "Here is your God! "See, the Sovereign Lord comes with power and his arm rules for him. See, his reward is with him, and his recompense accompanies him. He tends his flock like a shepherd: He gathers the lambs in his arms and carries them close to his heart; he gently leads those that have young." May the Lord bless this a portion from his holy word.

This is a passage which may or may not be familiar to many of us. It is one that has been set to music in Handel's Messiah. One of the most beautiful parts of Handel's Messiah is taken from this portion of the 40th chapter of Isaiah. But as we listen carefully to it we begin to wonder what in the world is happening here. We hear this phrase "wilderness and desert" and it makes us a little bit discomforted. It makes us a little bit concerned about what is being prophesied here. What is it Isaiah is hearing from God that he's trying to communicate with all of us. You see the wilderness concept is not one that is all that comfortable for most of us. To prepare a way for the Lord in the wilderness is not our idea of a good time to be had.

I was in Hobby Lobby with Debby a week or so ago and they had a sign there in their signage section and it showed this bear there, a big brown bear, and it said, "People in sleeping bags are just like soft tacos. "That's kind of what we think about with wilderness. That it is an "other" place, some place that you avoid, some place that you don't want to be. It's the kind of place that if you had to go to the wilderness, you'd say, "Let's take a nice camper with all the amenities of home and let's do it that way. "The thought of sleeping out in the wilderness is not, well, maybe it's me, there are probably a lot of people who would like to spend some time out in the wilderness and I did as a young man. I enjoyed sleeping out on the ground, under a tent and so on, that was a lot of fun. Over the years I realized the ground got harder, other discomforts started to set in so now I think it's roughing it if the hotel doesn't have a swimming pool.

But we hear Isaiah calling us to the wilderness in preparation for what God is going to do. We need to hear what is within that. Where else have we heard the term "wilderness" or in the "desert? "Well how about the 40 years the Israelites wandered in the wilderness? A time of preparation for them so when they got to the promised land they were fully ready to appreciate it and to receive it as the gift from God. Or how about the 40 days that Jesus spent in the wilderness being tempted in every way we human beings are. Or how about that character out of the Bible that we're not all that comfortable with? Our crazy Uncle John the Baptist. His proclamation of God's justice and righteousness in the wilderness was in preparation for Jesus' ministry and life and work among us.

So this idea of being sent to the wilderness is not one that should discomfort us but is one that offers to us a sense of God's working in our midst even in the most uncomfortable times and situations. That's certainly where we are right now. Would any of you say that 2020 has been a very comfortable year? Would any of you want to go back and do 2020 all over again? We are in the wilderness. And in that wilderness we need to prepare the way of the Lord. In that wilderness we need to prepare that way for the Lord to be more crucially a part of who we are and how we live our lives and how we look at the world around us, how we deal with other people. We are in the wilderness. But let us not forget the words that the prophet Isaiah started this passage with, this poetic passage that we find in the 40th chapter of Isaiah. "Comfort, comfort ye my people." It is to give us comfort. Now you have to understand too, that this is an imperative statement that is being made. It's not, "if you get a chance, it would be nice if you could comfort my people" or "if you are so inclined you could do something to comfort my people." It is an imperative, it is a command and not only is it in the imperative form, it is in the doubly imperative form. Whenever in the Hebrew language the use the same comparative twice, it means you better get it done. I always remember with my mom, she had that phrase "I've told you twice, if I have to tell you a third time, you're in trouble." Well that's what Isaiah is doing here. He is telling us that we are to be that comfort. That in our wilderness experience, in our transformation that takes place, in our preparation for what God is doing, in our participation with what God is doing, we are to be the comforters. We are to be the ones who bring comfort and hope and encouragement to everyone, everyone we meet, everyone we know, everyone we deal with.

Comfort, comfort ye my people. God speaks through Isaiah giving us our call that even in the wilderness of our lives, even in the discomfort of our lives we are to be the comforters, the ones who are doing God's work and God's will in this world. Prepare the way of the Lord. Be prepared for how God is working in and through us. Be prepared to hear again the wonder and the majesty and the mystery of the word become flesh and dwelling among us. Be prepared for the good news of Emmanuel, God with us. Be prepared to do God's work and to do God's will in this world where so much needs comfort and hope. Would you pray with me?

Our heavenly Father, we do give you thanks that even in the wilderness moments of our lives, you are an ever present help. Help us O Lord to be your comforters in this world, sharing the Good News of Jesus Christ through our words, through our actions, through our love, through our compassion. We pray this in Jesus' name and for his sake, Amen.

Pitching the Tent
2nd Samuel 7: 1-11, 16

December 20, 2020

I do want to say, just a point of personal privilege, as the phrase goes, that for those of you who follow the weather this past week, yes indeed, Binghamton, New York, where I lived for 20 years, yes indeed Conklin is right next to Binghamton, they got actually more snow than Binghamton did and friends of ours reported that they got close to four feet of snow at their home. So I'd like to take this moment to thank Gene Rosen and the rest of the PNC that brought me down here. If ever I was glad to be living here, this was the week. It was a wonderful place to live for all those years. A lot of beautiful attributes to that area and the snow is actually quite pretty until you have to move it, or get through it, or go around it or however you can make do with it. Yet it is a beautiful area to live and one of the beauties of that area is that they have some of the prettiest churches that you'll ever see. There's a church on Main Street on the west side in Binghamton called Tabernacle United Methodist Church, just a magnificent building, a beautiful sanctuary, it's got a Christian Education wing that's incredible and meeting spaces, I mean it's just a huge building. But I never did quite understand the name Tabernacle because a tabernacle is something that moves. A tabernacle is something that you take with you. We're going to hear a little bit more about that as we go on this morning but to build a large building that isn't going to move no matter what you do and calling it a tabernacle always seemed a little ironic to me! But building buildings to worship God is an old issue and we're going to take a look at that as well from II Samuel in the 7th chapter, the first 11 verses and then verse 16-17 also:

"After the king was settled in his palace and the Lord had given him rest from all his enemies around him, he said to Nathan the prophet, "Here I am living in a palace of cedar, while the ark of God remains in a tent. "Nathan replied to the king, "Whatever you have in mind, go ahead and do it, for the Lord is with

you. "That night the word of the Lord came to Nathan saying: "Go and tell my servant David, 'This is what the Lord says: Are you the one to build me a house to dwell in? I have not dwelt in a house from the day I brought the Israelites up out of Egypt to this day. I have been moving from place to place with a tent as my dwelling. Wherever I have moved with all the Israelites, did I ever say to any of their rulers whom I commanded to shepherd my people Israel, "Why have you not built me a house of cedar?"'" "Now then, tell my servant David, 'This is what the Lord Almighty says: I took you from the pasture and from following the flock to be ruler over my people Israel. I have been with you wherever you have gone, and I have cut off all your enemies from before you. Now I will make your name great, like the names of the greatest men of the earth. And I will provide a place for my people Israel and will plant them so that they can have a home of their own and no longer be disturbed. Wicked people will not oppress them anymore, as they did at the beginning and have done ever since the time I appointed leaders over my people Israel. I will give you rest from all your enemies.'" Your house and your kingdom will endure forever before me; your throne will be established forever. Nathan reported to David all the words of this entire revelation. May the Lord bless a portion from his holy word.

The Israelites were a part of their time and a part of their culture when David was king of Israel. Part of the culture around them was a misunderstanding of the deities, or in our understanding of the Deity. For most of the people around the people of Israel, their religions believed in multiple deities. They believed in a deity for every purpose and every situation. If you wanted crops to do well, you had a little god you could go to and pray for your crops. If you needed rain you could pray to the god of rain. If you needed sunshine, you could pray to the god of sunshine. If you wanted to have a large family you would pray to the god of fertility and so on and so on and so on. There was a god for every purpose that you can think of and every tribe every group had their own gods.

Another aspect of that was that they also believed that gods were local, that a god stayed in one place. This was a god of this town, this was the god of that town so you would have a god for all these purposes in this town, you would have gods for all these purposes in the next town, that all of the deities were localized - every community, every little tribe, every little gathering had their own personal gods and that if you moved from point A to point B, if you moved from Binghamton to Mechanicsville, you'd have to get a whole new set of gods because those gods were for that location. You needed to find out who the gods were for this location. And so, the understanding that they had was that was that god was in some way, shape, or form limited to being in one place - limited to being in one place at one time.

So, that was the understanding that the Israelites picked up from their neighbors, from the society around them. There was this understanding that God could only be in one place. And so they created the tabernacle and they carried God with them from place to place to place as they traveled through the wilderness, as they got settled in Israel, they were now faced with the issue of how can the king live in a beautiful cedar palace and we're keeping God in a tent outside.

So David wanted to make a correction to that. David wanted to fix that issue. David didn't like the thought that he was living in comfort and luxury and God was forced to stay outside in the rain so he was going to build God a palace, a temple in which to live. Nathan, a prophet, heard a word from God and the word basically comes down to this "I don't need a house, I don't need a dwelling place for wherever you are, I'm there with you. "Emmanuel - God with us. Nathan was trying to help David and for all the Israelites to see and to understand that God cannot be limited. God cannot be constrained. We cannot put God into a box and say, "here you go God, stay here. We'll call on you when we need you. Here you go God, something comfortable for you. Hope that means you'll treat me extra nice when I need the next favor from you. "God cannot be constrained. God cannot be held down, limited, kept in one place or in one manner. The one true God is the God who is with us wherever we go, whatever we do, whatever situation we might find ourselves in. God is there with us and for us. When things are going well, God is there with us. When things are going poorly, God is there with us. When we are able to worship together in a building, God is with us. When we are not able and we worship from our homes, God is with us.

This building is a house of God but God cannot be contained within this building. God is greater than all we can imagine and the thought of us constraining God or confining God into a space, time or even into a concept of who God is, is foolishness on our part. David had that desire to constrain God, to make sure that God was right there in this one place when David might need him. He wanted to confine God to one place so that David knew where to find him. But what David wasn't realizing was that God had found him not visa-versa. God is a God who is actively participating with us no matter where we go, no matter what we do, no matter what our situation may be, God is with us.

This is the truth that became so clear and evident as we make this transition during this week from Advent to Christmas, the presence of God with us became so clear and so real for us in the person of Jesus Christ. That Jesus came to be God's presence with us, to visually, tangibly show to us that God is with us. I know there's a lot of things happening in this world in which we live in that want to separate us from God - the discouragements of the times, the sacrifices we have made because of the Corona virus, the disappointments we have had, the plans that had to be broken, the dreams that have been put off to the side - all those things cannot keep God's presence away from us. God is with us. God is for us. God abides with us wherever we are. There's not any place where God is not present. The God whom we love, the God whom we serve is no minor deity. The God whom we love and we serve is greater that we can even imagine. His presence whose love, whose mercy, whose grace is an ever-present help in each of our lives no matter where we are or what our situation may be. Would you pray with me?

Almighty and ever-loving God, your love is unfathomable, your presence is so deeply needed and so deeply appreciated. Be with each and every one of us as we get through these days. Touch our hearts, touch our lives, fill us with your love, your grace and your mercy. We pray this in Jesus' name and for his sake. Amen.

Counting Your Blessings
Ephesians 1: 3 – 14

January 3, 2021

This is an odd Sunday in the life of the Christian church calendar. It is the second Sunday of Christmas. That's its technical name, it's also known as the Sunday before Epiphany, another role that this Sunday plays and it's also the first Sunday of a new year and so it is kind of a hybrid sort of Sunday. It's a Sunday that encompasses in a number of ways that we can go in looking at it and using it to help us to grow and understand our Christian faith. I thought that this being the year that it is, we all made it through 2020 and we're entered now into 2021, so that as I was talking to somebody before the early service and I wished them a Happy New Year, he said, "well I'm not wishing anyone Happy New Year at least until April. When I know how the year's going to go then I'll wish you a Happy New Year. I didn't do so good with last year's wishing people a Happy New Year. "

So, we are in a transition time, particularly this year maybe more so than any other year that has gone on before us, a transition between a year that most of us will be glad to forget and all of us were happy to say good-bye to. It wasn't a year that any of us will mark as a great year for us as a community, a church, a nation or a world. It was one of those years that took its toll upon us and shaped us in many ways; maybe not in ways we wanted to be shaped and maybe not in ways that we're happy to be shaped.

So I was thinking about the first Sunday in a new year; a time of transition for us and this passage from Ephesians seemed to be appropriate to me. Let me read it for you and let's see what Paul can help us to see as we go into a new year. From Paul's letter to the church of Ephesus, in the first chapter, and I'm going to read verses 3-16. I know it's a lot to read and I already have somebody out there shaking her head "no" at me reading this many verses but it's too hard to break this up and I think we need to see the whole of it to get the most out of it.

"Blessed be the God and Father of our Lord Jesus Christ, who has blessed us in Christ with every spiritual blessing in heavenly places. Just as he chose us in Christ, before the foundation of the world to be holy and blameless before him in love. He destined us for adoption as his children through Jesus Christ according to his good pleasure and will - to the praise of his glorious grace, which he has freely bestowed on us in the beloved one. In him we have redemption through his blood, the forgiveness of our trespasses according to the riches of his grace that he lavished on us with all wisdom and insight he has made known to us the mystery of his will according to his good pleasure that he set forth in Christ as a plan for the fullness of time to gather up all things in him, things in heaven and things on earth. In Christ we have also obtained an inheritance having been destined according to the purpose of him who accomplishes all things according to his counsel and will so that we who were the first to set our hope on Christ might live for the praise of his glory. In him you also, when you had heard the word of truth, the gospel of your salvation and had believed in him were marked with a seal of the promised Holy Spirit. This is the pledge of our inheritance towards redemption as God's own people. To the praise of his glory, I have heard of your faith in the Lord Jesus and your love toward all the saints and for this reason I do not cease to give thanks for you as I remember you in my prayers. 'May the Lord bless this, a portion from his holy word.

Giving thanks, being grateful, looking on the bright side, good watch words for the beginning of a new year but not words that come easily or naturally to us at this point in our lives. Now, I have to admit that this may not be a sermon for all of you. This may not be a sermon that I'm preaching to you as much as it is a sermon that I am preaching for myself because it is so hard right now to really be positive, it is hard right now to truly be grateful, to count our blessings. It is not an easy time to have that attitude in my heart and in my life because there's a lot of things I'm missing right now. There's a lot of that I long for right now. There's a lot of things that I just as soon get rid of right now. I mean, all of the traditions around Christmas this year, traditions that I love and I enjoy, I relish, that I long for, that I look forward to, so many of those traditions were changed or taken away in this season that we are in right now. I mean, I love being here on Christmas Eve and preaching to a packed house. Yes, I do worry about those candles and people getting too close to each other with the candles, but there's nothing more beautiful than seeing this sanctuary of people shoulder to shoulder, chairs in the aisle, chairs in the hallway and chairs any place we can put chairs and hearing that singing and then this year we didn't get to do that. We moved to the Family Center because it made sense for spacing and other reasons. It just was the safer option and no candles because we couldn't figure out to blow out a candle with a mask on your face. I tried, trust me, I tested every way I could figure out and I blew and I blew as hard as I could and it didn't even make the flame flicker. And then, at home, usually we put all the Christmas presents under the tree and to me that one of the prettiest sights in the world as all the presents under the tree but not this year because we were protecting Courtney and Miheer and Chad and Lindley, we put the presents at appropriate seats far enough away from each other We all sat in our little corners and had our presents to open up that were right in front of us and that was nice, it was wonderful and presents were great and it was nice to be together but I missed the chaos of it! Usually it was Courtney who was sent to pull the presents from under the tree, "whose that one for? " I get all excited and watch that person opening up a present and it was chaotic but I missed it. We didn't have that and I can't even hug my daughter right now just because of our being cautious with COVID. I could go on and list so many more ways and if I started a list I have a hunch that you could join with me in making that list even longer - the things that we don't have, the things that we miss, the things that we long for and experiences that we didn't have and so on. We could probably spend a good 20 minute sermon just lamenting the things that we are missing right now and complaining about the things that we have to endure right now: you know what I'm talking about.

But then we hear the Apostle Paul writing to the church of Ephesus and we hear all of these positive words that he's speaking; words of gratitude, words of thanksgiving, words that have such a wonderful positive spirit to them, much to be grateful for, blessings being counted and you know the first reaction is we think: you know "it's Paul. "Paul was a great apostle and let me just tell you this as an aside, David is my oldest brother's second child and in my family we all had biblical first names. As so it started off with Paul then John, my sister Miriam, and then myself. Now I always grew up feeling kind of cheated because Paul, the great apostle, John, the gospel writer, the oracle of the Book of Revelation and. . . Stephen the martyr at a young age. I never felt that was fair.

But you think about Paul and you think about all the things that he accomplished, the great apostle, the establisher of so many churches, the one who was given credit for the spread of Christianity throughout the world, the one who took what Christ had done and shared it with the Gentiles - took it from being a Jewish sect to being a religion that is open to all people and to all places, all times, all languages and so on. What he accomplished in his lifetime was incredible. So you read a passage like this and you think well that's fine for Paul, he had it all going for him. He was one of the greats and we know his name 2,000 years later. But then you think a little bit more about that and you quickly begin to remember that maybe it wasn't so good for Paul. Maybe it wasn't so easy for him. I mean, he wrote this toward the last third of his ministry and by that time he had been imprisoned innumerable times, he had been thrown out of every synagogue you can imagine, he had been shipwrecked, he had so much bad happen to him, I mean, he was hungry, he was cold, If it could go wrong, it did go wrong for the Apostle Paul. So here he is, this one who had so much happening to him that was so negative: that makes wearing a silly little mask seem inconsequential.

He's writing all of this, giving thanks to God for all the blessings that he has received, giving thanks to God for the church at Ephesus for their faithfulness in Christ's work. And this is not just some little side note that he's giving because letters in that day had a certain format. We have a format for how we write letters nowadays, we have our letterhead or the address from which it's coming, the address for where it's going, the date, dear such and such I hope this letter finds you well, and then the content of the letter, then sincerely and you sign your name and so on. We have a format. They had a format back then. It usually started off with a quick identification in this case Paul, Apostle of Christ Jesus by the will of God and then to whom it is written, then it always includes some kind words or kind remembrances usually a sentence or two, maybe a short paragraph and Paul goes on where we delineate it here as a full chapter on his gratitude and all he is grateful for from God, from the people of Ephesus and so on. He is zealous in his thanksgiving. He has recognized that in spite of all of the things that have gone wrong in his life, in spite of all setbacks, in spite of the imprisonments, in spite of all the persecution, in spite of being rejected and cast out and almost being killed and so on, in spite of all of that, he sees so much to be grateful for. So many blessings to count in his life.

Now, I don't generally get my theology from country and western songs but I'm going to make an exception. There's a song out right now that I think is entitled "We Had it All" that goes on in the song to say we had it all when we had nothing at all and talks about his childhood and how they were poor as a church mouse and didn't have anything but yet in those moments they had it all. They had love. They had love. That's what the Apostle Paul is saying to us in this opening passage of his letter to the church of Ephesus. You and I have it all. We have the love of God. Time and time again he words and rewords it and rewords it again but it always comes down to this: that you and I are blessed because we are loved by God. That God has chosen to love us. He has chosen us to be his sons and daughters. Now that is important point to note because God could have chosen differently. God could have looked at this world that he created and he could have said, "Well, I bollixed that one up. They're selfish, self-centered, they're going every direction but the way they ought to be going. You know what, forget them. I got a whole huge universe. I can start with another planet somewhere else. " But God chose instead to never give up on us. God chose instead to love us with an unconditional love, to love us with an infinite love, to love us in a way, in a manner that goes beyond anything that we could ever hope or expect from God. If we have God's love, if we have that love in our hearts and in our minds and in our lives then we have it all, we have it all. The little things that we endure right now, the limitations that are placed upon us are nothing when compared to the love of God we see and experience in Jesus Christ.

This table that stands before us today is such a tangible reminder of that truth. It's the truth of the depth and the breath; the height of God's love for each and every one of us. There is nothing that God wouldn't do to be in relationship with us. There is no end to where God would not go in order to have us be his sons and daughters, not even death upon the cross through his son Jesus Christ, is too much for him to do for you and for me. This meal is a simple, tangible reminder of God's infinite love toward each and every one of us. To taste, to experience, to enjoy, to be reminded. "Do this in remembrance of me" Jesus said. And what we are remembering in remembering him is that infinite love toward each and every one of us.

In this new year, in 2021, there are no guarantees that it's going to be any better than 2020. But there is the guarantee that no matter what we have God's love in our lives. If we have that love, we have it all. Would you pray with me?

Almighty and ever-loving God, it's hard to comprehend the avenues to which you have gone to love us, to forgive us, to welcome us home as your sons and daughters. Help us O Lord in this new year to be a grateful people counting our blessings, the blessing of being loved by you. We pray all this in Jesus' name. Amen.

God Created
Genesis 1: 1-5

January 10, 2021

We're going to begin a new series of sermons "Created Anew", on the God who creates and the implications of that and what that means for us and how that helps us to look at the world in which we live - how that helps us to see and understand our responsibility within this world. And so, we begin the sermon series in a logical and reasonable place . . . at the beginning. Genesis chapter 1, the first five verses there.

"In the beginning God created the heavens and the earth. Now the earth was formless and empty, darkness was over the surface of the deep, and the Spirit of God was hovering over the waters. And God said, "Let there be light," and there was light. God saw that the light was good, and he separated the light from the darkness. God called the light "day," and the darkness he called "night. "And there was evening and there was morning - for the first day. 'May the Lord bless this a portion from his holy word.

Now, for us in the 21st century, in the western hemisphere, more particularly in these United States of America, Genesis chapter 1 and chapter 2 have always been a bit of a perplexing problem for us. You see, we have a mindset, we have a way of looking at things that seemingly commands us to ask questions along the lines of "how? ". We want to know how things work. We want to know how things transpired. We want to know how it is that God did what God did. How long was a day? This debate has been going on as long as I've been around and still goes on - whether it was seven 24 hour days, whether it was seven eons , seven units of time that we don't measure with anymore, what was it, how did all of that work, how did God do what God did in the creation of the heavens and the earth? We want to know. That's our mindset, that's our training, that's our academic background, that's our scholarly way of doing things: it is to think in a scientific manner: A+B'C,step one leads to step two which creates step 3. We want to know how all of those pieces of the puzzle fall together. That's how we generally look at Genesis and we try and figure out how does this all fit together? How did God do that?

Now, to be honest with you, that is an exercise in futility because the writer of Genesis and the Hebrew people who first knew God and who have shared God with us, the people to whom God revealed himself, the people of God adopted as his own, for the benefit of the world, never thought about those kinds of questions. They did not think in the same manner as we think. They were not concerned with the "hows? "They were concerned with the "whos. "When the writer is sharing with all of us that "in the beginning God created the heavens and the earth", he is not writing a scientific textbook of the "hows" of creation. He is desiring to share with us the person who would create. The most important thing for the Hebrew writer of Genesis is who created the heavens and the earth. And the answer is proclaimed loudly and clearly throughout the first and second chapters of Genesis. It is God who is the actor? It is God who is the creator? It is God who spoke and day and night came into being? It is God who spoke and life began to appear? For the writer of Genesis, the number one question is answered in the statement - In the beginning **God** created the heavens and the earth.

But they were also concerned with what that tells us about this God. What does this action tell us about the person and work of God? And the answer is God is one who creates, who makes something good. That tells us a lot about the person of God. That tells us what God's goals and desires and hopes and dreams were. For God created all of this beauty to be enjoyed, he created people to enjoy relationships, he created the animals to serve us and for us to serve them to live as a peaceable kingdom on this planet that he spun out of nothing. It tells us a lot about God. It tells us a lot about what God's desires are for each and every one of us, what his hopes and dreams and expectations are for you and for me.

When I lived in Wyalusing, just outside of Wyalusing was a small town (not that Wyalusing was a big town) called Le Raysville and in the farming community surrounding Le Raysville was a large Amish population there. They had bought up a number of farms so they could move out from Lancaster County in Pennsylvania up to northern Pennsylvania where land was affordable. They took over farms that had gone bankrupt and farms that weren't workable anymore and they took these farms and made them workable, made them profitable and they did all sorts of other things as well. They had a cheese plant where they made wonderful cheese. They made baked goods that did not help my slim trim figure that I entered Wyalusing with. They did carpentry that was extraordinary. They did all these sorts of things. They were a tremendous asset to the community of Bradford County in Pennsylvania, what wonderful, wonderful people.

Well, the church in Wyalusing (and I may have told you this before) was given a four-story hotel that was right next to the church - I don't think it was more than twelve feet distance between the two buildings. The hotel towered over the church but it had deteriorated terribly. It's a long story but there was no redeeming this old beautiful gothic structure. (There were trees growing on the third floor -never a good sign!)So, when we were given that building, the church tried to think of some way to save it but nobody had a budget big enough to save that building. Therefore, we made the difficult decision to have the building torn down. We put it out to bid. We got three bids back, two local construction companies were willing to do it. I know this isn't going to sound like a lot of money but in 1982-83 it was a lot of money. The two bids from the construction companies came back at $30,000 and $35,000, respectively, to take down the Middendorf Hotel. But we got a third bid from an Amish crew, headed by a young man named Eli Miller and their bid was $15,000 - half of the next highest bid. Well, there were people around the table at the session meeting who said, "That's well and good. It would be nice to save $15,000 but how in the world are they going to do this? They don't use heavy equipment, they don't use power equipment of any way, shape or kind. How are they going to do this?" But one of the elders, a fellow by the name of Roy Jones said, "Well let's do this: rather than just pass on their bid, let's ask them to come in and meet with us and tell us how they are going to do it. "And so, Eli came the next week, sat with us around the table and he was asked a bunch of questions and finally somebody said, "You don't use power tools, how in the world are you going to take down a building like that?" He said, "When it was built they didn't have the power tools we have today. What we're planning to do is just do everything they did in the 1800's when they built it except we're going to do it in reverse." They got the bid. We hired them to take down the Middendorf Hotel for us and it was an incredible experience. They were so methodical on everything that they did. As they left at the end of every day you couldn't find a nail on the ground, they cleaned up after themselves, it was like nothing was happening in there. They did such a good job.

In the course of that time, as they were taking down the hotel, I got to know Eli a little bit and we had some very good conversations and I really wanted to learn more about his faith and what made them the kind of people they were. One of the things that has always stuck in my mind in talking with Eli was that their first preference is always to be farmers for the theological reason that when they are farming they're co-creators with God. They're picking up and continuing the work that God began in the beginning. They saw that as the highest calling to be co-creators with God, to do God's work in this world, to be one who brings something seemingly out of nothing for the good and the benefit of others. And that was absolutely true because if they couldn't be farmers, they were bakers and they were creators of beautiful quilts and other things and if they couldn't do that, they were carpenters who were building homes and building other kinds of structures. They were all very much into being creative, building up, making something good and even as they took down the Middendorf, a four-story structure, (I don't know how many square feet were in that four-story big old hotel,) they took one truck to the dump. Everything else they reused. They even separated the wood lathe from the old horse-hair plaster. They bundled the wood lathe to be used as kindling and they took the old horsehair plaster to be used as fertilizer in their fields. They were very much desirous of being ones who were participants in God's creation, being co-creators with God.

In Genesis, as we see what it is that God desires of us, it comes down to that as well. For the Amish, Eli Miller, his crew, his community, they got it right. We are to be a positive addition to the world. To do things that build up, that are constructive, that are positive, that are creative, that make the world a better place, make the world more like the way God intended it to be. We're called to be co-creators. The New Testament uses a phrase time and time again "to edify" which means to build up or it could mean to be constructive, that we are called to be ones who build up one another, who are constructive in our relationships with each other, that we are ones who are constructive in the world in which we live. And that's the call of the church - to be a constructive people, a people who build up in this world, and we seem to have lost that clarion call on our life together and our lives individually.

One of the curses or blessings of so many services being on-line as we are is it gives me an opportunity to see what others are doing, how others are preaching, what their services are like and so on which is good. I mean it's good to learn from others and improve how we do things here, what I've seen is a polarity happening within the Christian church. A polarity that is, instead of reflecting God to the world is reflecting the world back to our faith. What I mean is that I have heard sermons on one side of the theological spectrum who feel that if we have this president in place, if we have this party in control, then the Kingdom of God will be at hand. And I've heard others on the other side of the theological spectrum saying if we get this person into the presidency, this party controls the government, then the Kingdom of God will be at hand, we will have done our part if this party or that party is the party that is in power and in control then all will be well in the world and the Kingdom of God will be at hand. And how has that been working this year? There's been more destruction in the streets of America in the last twelve months than any of us have seen in many, many, years. The call of the church is not in destruction. The call of the church is not in tearing other people down. The call of the church is to build one another up. The Kingdom of God will never be found in the Republican party or in the Democrat party or any party in-between. The Kingdom of God is found when we learn how to live with one another, to love one another, to build up one another. We need to learn how to be creative in our communication to such a degree that we learn how to listen to one another instead of waiting for our turn to talk. The church needs to call ourselves and our country back to being a constructive people. Getting away from that which is destructive and moving toward that which builds up, edifies, creates good in this world and you don't do it by destroying one another. We don't do it by destroying buildings and businesses, windows and statues, being destructive at the nations' Capitol - all sorts of things that have been destroyed in this past twelve months.

In the beginning God created the heavens and the earth. God calls us to join him in that creation to be a people who can look and see what we have accomplished and honestly say to ourselves, it is good. Would you pray with me?

Almighty and ever-loving heavenly Father, forgive us for our destruction. Forgive us when we think that power is what we should desire the most. O heavenly Father, help us to follow in your footsteps, to be a people who are co-creators with you, people who build up, who edify, who are constructive, who make this world a better place through love, through grace, through compassion, through mercy, through peace. We pray this all in Jesus' name and for his sake, Amen.

Creating Christian Freedom
I Corinthians 6: 12 – 20

January 17, 2021

Thank you Donna (Horn). That was just beautiful and it's funny how a song can transport you to different places and different times and that one always takes me back to my Dad. That was one of my Dad's favorite hymns. He first heard it and I think this is how it became popular in the United States with a Billy Graham Evangelistic broadcast. That was the first time it was heard in the United States and Dad fell in love with it at that moment and figured out how to get the music and introduced it to the congregation. He got himself in trouble with the congregation because they didn't want to learn a new hymn. The irony is that the woman who screamed loudest at my dad about introducing a new hymn and that she didn't want to be singing new hymns in her church, she wanted the old favorites, the one hymn she requested for her funeral was How Great Thou Art. What a beautiful hymn it is and how blessed we are to have you sing it Donna. Thank you.

We're going to continue in our series of sermons on God's creation or God as creator and it's not what you might think of the sermon series to be. It's not centered around the beauty of God's creation and the wonders of God's creation but really more along the lines of the fact that the God who is the creator, continues to create and that we as sons and daughters of our heavenly Father are part of that continuing creation, that we are being made anew, that God is creating us into whom we are being called to be. And so we're going to be looking at that in terms of the question *how are we created anew?* In the passage that Darren read for us from II Corinthians, that if we are in Christ then we are a *new* creation. What does that mean? How does that look? How are we different because of Christ's presence in our lives? How are we different because of what Jesus Christ has done for each one of us?

Well that was a question on the minds of the early church as well and they were struggling to figure that out and the one thing that they latched on to very well is what it does for them personally. If we are in Christ then we are forgiven people. We are people whose sins have been washed away. We are people that there is nothing that we can do that will separate us from the love of God. There is nothing that we can do that God will not forgive us because of what Christ has done in paying the penalty for us. And so, it was a question in the early church "then what does that mean? How is it that we ought to live or maybe the question that they were really asking was how is it can live? "Kind of like kids: what can we get away with?

I'd like us to look at a text from I Corinthians in the sixth chapter, verses 12-29. I don't want you to get stuck on the example that he's dealing with here. I don't want you getting stuck on the particular matter that he's dealing with here because it does kind of catch our attention and grab us but I want us to look beyond the particular matter and see what it is that we need to understand about what it means to be forgiven sons and daughters of our heavenly Father.

"Everything is permissible for me" - but not everything is beneficial. "Everything is permissible for me" - but I will not be mastered by anything. "Food for the stomach and the stomach for food" - but God will destroy them both. The body is not meant for sexual immorality, but for the Lord, and the Lord for the body. By his power God raised the Lord from the dead, and he will raise us also. Do you not know that your bodies are members of Christ himself? Shall I then take the members of Christ and unite them with a prostitute? Never! Do you not know that he who unites himself with a prostitute is one with her in body? For it is said, "The two will become one flesh. "But he who unites himself with the Lord is one with him in spirit. Flee from sexual immorality. All other sins a man commits are outside the body, but he who sins sexually sins against his own body. Do you not know that your body is a temple of the Holy Spirit, who is in you, whom you have received from God? You are not your own; you were bought at a price. Therefore honor God with your body. ' May the Lord bless this a portion from his holy word.

The church at Corinth was not a good church. It was not a strong church, it was not a healthy church, it was a struggling church. It was under that category that if I were looking for a new church to serve and the Corinth church offered me the pastorate, it would be a hard no thank you. It seemed as if they were struggling with the question of *what does it mean to be a forgiven person?* What does it mean to be a follower of Jesus Christ and to know that there is nothing that we can do that will undo the forgiveness that we have received? And they thought that meant that everything was permissible. "Everything is lawful for me" was the phrase that was used and we believed that's Paul quoting something they had from them when he uses that phrase and as a matter of fact most of the translations put that phrase in quotation marks because we think that Paul is responding to something that someone had written to him from the church at Corinth making that statement. They believed that since we are forgiven people and that whatever we do, whatever we have done, whatever we do, whatever we will do that is sinful, that God will forgive it because of what Christ has done for us. And so therefore there is nothing we can do that is going to separate us from the love of God therefore we can do whatever we please, or maybe more specific whatever pleases us. They end up in this situation that they are continuing on doing things that they did previously to being followers of Jesus Christ. One of the stronger religious groups in Corinth, (and I had trouble trying to describe this earlier, Darren would not help me. He just sat there and laughed.)But one of the stronger religious groups in Corinth, part of their religious ritual involved the use of prostitutes. Some in the early church who came out of that religious persuasion and into the Christian faith continued to involve themselves in that ritual out of their former tradition. Now, you and I could look at that and we know immediately that they were not doing that action as a self-discipline or a spiritual discipline. This was not a religious ritual that they were doing to better themselves. You and I look at that and go, "yes, there are other reasons why they were doing that, that had nothing to do with the religious faith. "It was all about what they wanted.

It was all about the fact if we are forgiven as Christians that we can do anything we want and so their decision making process became clouded because they enveloped themselves in the world of me.

What is it that is best for me? What is it that pleases me? What is it that makes me happy? And they lost the fact that as followers of Jesus Christ we are a new creation. We are not who we once were without Christ. We are not who we would be had we not known Christ's love in our lives. One of the things of being a new creation is that now we are connected with Jesus. We are not living for ourselves anymore. Certainly we are forgiven and certainly there is nothing we can do that would separate us from God's love in Jesus Christ. But we have to make that movement from "me" to "we. "It's not a natural motion. It is not the way that is ingrained in us. It's not the way of the society in which we live right now. For we live in a society that is all about "me. "All about what is best for me. All about what I want, when I want it and how I want it. That's what the society around us is saying. That is what the society around us is practicing. You don't have to look very far to see that's absolutely true. You can go to any number of lengths to look at things to think about and go, "yeah, we are living in a very selfish period of time. "If you go on to social media and I don't do that very much at all because it just drives me crazy but if you go on to social media you'll see conversations happening there and one of the most common conversations that I've heard in the last five or six months is, "this is what I think- if you don't agree with me I'm going to un-friend you. I'm not going to be your friend anymore if you disagree with me because I'm right and you're wrong. End of discussion. "That's pretty selfish. That's not seeing in others the image of God. That's not seeing in others the goodness that God sees in them. That is absolutely selfishness to the nth degree. But that self-centeredness, me centeredness is very, very natural for us.

Let me tell you this. I've always had a hands-off policy when it comes to who is called to be an elder or a deacon or any other office in the church. I always step back from the nominating committee. I don't take part in it in any way shape or form unless they come and ask me a question. Other than that, I have no part of it. It was a good number of years ago when the nominating committee presented their slate for the upcoming year's elections and on it was a name that I dreaded seeing on there. This person was the thorn in my flesh.

If I said up, he said down. If I said left, he said right. If I said this is good, he said this is bad. And I bit my tongue that evening at the meeting but when I got home poor Debby heard an earful from me. "I can't believe they're going to do this to me. This is going to be the worst three years of my life, it's going to be terrible to have him on session, I don't know what they were thinking, they should have asked me. . . " and I just whined and moped and whined and poor Debby had probably more than she could deal with that. But, I kept hands off. He was elected, became part of the session and he was one of the best elders I've ever served with. He was just a hard working person, he had wisdom, insight, he saw things the rest of us missed and he brought energy and enthusiasm, intelligence, imagination and love to the table. All the things you would want out of an elder and he was one of the best I have ever worked with. Now the "me" would have said keep him off the session. That would have been my first wish, that would have been what I wanted but as Christians we are called to think about the "we" to look at others and to see how God loves them as well. To get out of ourselves and see in others the goodness that God sees in them as well.

It doesn't matter how they might be different from us or how they might differ from us. We are called to love one another in the same selfless way that Jesus Christ lived his life. Can you think of any example out of Jesus' life where he chose his own self-interest over the interest of others? I certainly can't. Jesus always chose the interest of others over against his own self-interest even to be willing to die on the cross. Not for anything he had done, not for anything he would gain but he died on the cross for you and for me. Selfless living - all things are permissible. There is nothing that we can do that will separate us from the love of God. There is nothing that we can do that God will not forgive us but that doesn't mean we should do anything for selfish reasons. It means that we are now part of the body of Christ and we ought to reflect in our lives that same love that Jesus himself exemplified in his life. If we do it right, if we live our lives as a new creation, if we allow Christ to be center of our lives, then we don't have to answer any of these questions anymore. If we live as Christ-centered people then those around us will not see us, they'll see Jesus instead. If we live our lives as Christ-centered people, people who are created anew because of Christ's love for us, then we will see in others, no matter how different they may be, no matter how much we might differ from them, we will see in them what Christ sees in them as well. All things are lawful, all things are permissible but we should be seeking what is beneficial, what is good not for ourselves, but what is good for others.

Would you pray with me?

O heavenly Father, forgive us. Forgive us for our natural attitude that somehow or another thinks that we are the center of the universe. Forgive us for our natural attitude that thinks that what we want is what we should have. Help us, O Lord, to put Jesus first. Help us O Lord to see in others the good that you see in them. Help us O Lord to put ourselves last so that we might reflect your love to those who are around us. O gracious Lord, help us indeed to be your new creations, to be your people - your sons and daughters and help us to live in that manner. We pray this in Jesus' name and for his sake. Amen.

Never-Ending Creativity
Isaiah 40: 21 – 31

February 7, 2021

Thank you for those who are here today, being present, I know it's a small number. Kind of reminds me of the story of a group of women were meeting together for a cup of tea and the discussion turned to the size of their particular congregations. They were all talking about how small their congregations were and then one woman says, "well I think my church is the smallest," They said, "Really? "She says, "Oh yes. Mine is so small that every time the minister says 'dearly beloved', I blush. "So we have that smallness about us but I know that there are many more who are watching from the safety and security of their homes and we're glad to have all of you with us as well. It's pretty looking outside but it's kind of a miserable day nonetheless with the road conditions and the concerns that we have with all that.

You know we feel like we're living in a miserable time with Covid-19 and everything else going on and we know that's what exactly the Israelites were going through. They were live in a horribly miserable time in their existence when the prophet Isaiah was speaking to the people. They were in exile as in exilic period. They were brought out by the Babylonians and taken away from everything that they knew and loved and cherished: traditions, places, everything was taken away from them and they felt lost in this world. They also felt, in a very real sense, that they had been abandoned by their God. It was a miserable time for them, a miserable experience for them and then Isaiah comes to them with some words for them to hear. In this 40th chapter of Isaiah is one of the most beautiful poems- it's a poetic word that he received from God. When you get home today and you want to pull out your Bible and read the entire 40th chapter of Isaiah, it is poetic in its nature. There is something special about poetry that says things in a way that the regular spoken word doesn't. Prose just can't touch what poetry can do maybe that's why music is so special for us because it is poetry that we have attached some musical notes. That speaks to our hearts and that's exactly what Isaiah was trying to do for the Israelites as they were in a miserable experience in their lives. In some ways, not exactly in the same way as they did, you know what they experienced is nothing like what we're experiencing but in some small way we feel right now as if we are in an exilic period. We are away from those traditions, those experiences, those opportunities that have made our lives rich. They have been taken away from us by this COVID19. So we live in an exilic period ourselves in a different way, in a different fashion, not nearly as drastic as what the Israelites did but in some ways I also know that we are like the Israelites in the fact that there's a part of us that wants to blame God. There's a part of us that feels as if God has abandoned us and we're all on our own in the midst of this exilic period in which we find ourselves living.

Let's take a look then. Let's listen to what the prophet Isaiah said and I'm going to pick up at the 21st verse of the 40th chapter and hear what Isaiah knew that God wanted the Israelites and us to hear:

Do you now know? Have you not heard? Has it not been told you from the beginning? Have you not understood since the earth was founded? He sits enthroned above the circle of the earth, and its people are like grasshoppers. He stretches out the heavens like a canopy, and spreads them out like a tent to live in. He brings princes to naught and reduces the rulers of the world to nothing. No sooner are they planted, no sooner are they sown, no sooner do they take root in the ground, than he blows on them and they wither, and a whirlwind sweeps them away like chaff.

"To whom will you compare me? Or who is my equal?" says the Holy One. Lift your eyes and look to the heavens: Who created all these? He who brings out the starry host one by one, and calls them each by name. Because of his great power and mighty strength, not one of them is missing.

Why do you say, O Jacob, and complain, O Israel, "My way is hidden from the Lord; my cause is disregarded by my God"? Do you not know? Have you not heard? The Lord is the everlasting God, the Creator of the ends of the earth. He will not grow tired or weary, and his understanding no one can fathom. He gives strength to the weary and increases the power of the weak. Even youths grow tired and weary, and young men stumble and fall; but those who hope in the Lord will renew their strength. They will soar on wings like eagles; they will run and not grow weary, they will walk and not be faint. May the Lord bless us a portion from his holy word.

It does feel like we're in exile doesn't it? We're missing so many things, so many opportunities, so many gatherings. Remember that phrase "gatherings? "Being together with people we miss, the handshakes, the hugs, the times of being close with people, we miss the many, many opportunities that make our lives a little richer and more special. We have lost so much because of this COVID19 and it is wearing us down at this point. We're about hitting the one-year mark when the word COVID came into our vocabulary and we're tired of this and we don't know where it will end. We're not sure what it will look like when it is all over. Will there be some declaration from somebody in the governor's office or somebody in Washington who is going to say, "okay folks all at once now take off those masks. "Or will it come a little bit at a time? Will it come soon? Or will it come later? We don't know these answers and we are feeling bereft, we are feeling as if we are lost at sea and not sure where the horizon of the land is and we question God's presence in all of this. We start to see everything from our own personal perspective. We start to see everything from just our own self vision: what I have lost, what I am missing, what I am longing for. We start to see things from just that personal perspective: we can't see beyond the stretch of our own hands. That's where the Israelites were. They had no idea when their exile would end. Would anything ever be the same again? Are we going to have to live with the new normal? Questions the Israelites were raising from their perspective of what they had lost, what they were missing. Then the prophet Isaiah comes along and smacks them in the side of the head and says, "Don't you remember? Have you forgotten that God alone is God and you are not. Have you forgotten that it is God who places the stars in the heavenly skies and knows each star by its name? Have you forgotten that God is the creator who is so far above us that our understanding of him is very vague and faint. "

But then I see it gives us one verse to cling to, that 31st verse: "But those who wait for the Lord shall renew their strength, they shall mount up with wings like eagles they shall run and not be weary they shall walk and not be faint. " and we hear that passage in we cling to because we all want to be eagles, do we not? We all want to soar above this. That's the first offer he gives to us - to be able to fly. Why does he offer us the ability to fly? When I was a teenager good friend of mine, Danny Harkenreader was a young pilot, he was a couple years older than I and he had achieved his private pilot's license. But he was seeking to get his commercial pilot's license which meant that he needed to get a lot of hours in the air. So, what he would do to make it affordable and to allow us an opportunity, his circle of friends would be invited to fly with him in his small Cessna that he would rent out of the Carbondale-Clifford Airport. We would fly with Danny as he would get his hours. There is nothing like it. Flying in big planes is fine if you like to feel like a sardine but if you want to see the world, a small plane is the way to go. You're at a fairly low altitude, you have a window view no matter which way you look and you get to see things from a different perspective. I remember flying with Danny and we will fly over the little villages and towns and small cities of Northeastern Pennsylvania and you would go, "look there's Clifford! There's Carbondale! I think that's Dundaff down there! " You would get a whole different perspective on each of those little towns! You would fly over the different mountain ridges and you would start to name them by name because you could see them from a whole different perspective. "There's Elk mountain over there! There's Salem Mountain over here! " You had a whole different perspective than you can get when you are on the ground looking around because what kind of perspective do we have down here? It's a very limited perspective.

God offers us to rise-up as if on eagles wings so that we might gain a better perspective on what is happening, to be able to look around and to be reminded that God is God and God is in control and the God who is in control is the God who loves us, the God who loves us and is able to bring out of even the worst of situations something good. That's a promise he has made and that's a promise he has fulfilled time and time again. So, God seeks to lift us up on eagle's wings - not so that we can move from point A to point B but so that we can get a better perspective: a more holistic perspective- a more holy perspective on our lives and on the world in which we are living.

He says we can run and not be weary. I'll tell you something that should be obvious to all of you, I am not a runner. I do not run. I have not run. I will not run. (It sounds like a Dr. Seuss book is starting here.)I mean even when I was a young fellow and I know this is part you are not going to believe but at 17 years of age I was 5 feet 11 3/4 inches and 135 pounds. I was scrawny, thin as a rail, a good stiff wind I was two counties away. Even then I did not run. Occasionally I would run if it was required for a sporting event. If I was playing baseball, running to first base, fine, I'll do that but even then it was not with great enthusiasm or energy. I remember one time we were playing Church softball on a co-ed team and I hit a line drive that went right down the first base line got past the right fielder went all the way into the tall grass that was just beyond the mowed area of the outfield. I was running, I was running. I got down to first base, I made the corner and I turned toward second baseman looked to my right. I saw the outfielder had gotten to the ball and I thought well I'll just go back to first base and be careful and safe. I didn't think much about it but after that half inning I got back to the bench to get my glove and one of my fellow players, she says to me, "Steve I've never seen anybody stretch a triple into a single before. "So, running is not my thing. It's not that is not a good thing and for those who run for exercise and for their health: you have my deepest admiration. I'd like to say envy you, but I won't. It is a good thing to do and it's a healthy thing to do but it's not how we live our lives day in and day out. I watched as you all came into the sanctuary this morning. I did not see one of you running to get in here. I may see you running to get out but that's another story. That's not the way that we live. Running is not our natural way of living from day to day. It is something that we do in urgent situations. We might run to avoid something, we might run to catch something, we might run in all sorts of little situations that call for that extra burst of energy. In those cases what God is saying through Isaiah is that in those times in your life when you have to reach down in deep and dig for something extra, I'll be your strength. It won't wear you out, I've got you covered. We live through those moments where we feel as if we are running but even in those moments God is with us and will not allow us to be weary.

You might think that the prophet Isaiah got these things out of order. You might think that it should have been in the other direction. You might think it should have built up to the crescendo of walking, running, flying. But I think that the writer heard God clearly and got it in the right order because the final promise of walking and not fainting is the promise that we need the most because walking is how we live our lives. Walking is the normal average way of doing what we need to do. We walk out to the kitchen to get a snack. We walk upstairs to take our evenings rest. We walk around the grocery store to pick up our groceries. We walk as a normal activity and what the prophet Isaiah is helping us to see is that no matter what our situation is, our day-to-day lives, our coming, our going, our average moments are where God is with us and for us, we will walk and not grow faint. We will do the normal average regular sorts of things that we have to do, and it won't wear us out because God is there with us and for us holding us up and carrying us along.

The Israelites wanted answers. The Israelites wanted times and dates, the means and methods of the end of their exile and instead they got a promise of God's presence. No matter where they were, no matter what they were doing, they got a promise of God's overarching perspective that ultimately God is in control and we are not. They got the promise of God's walking with them and holding them up along the way. We would love to know: April 15, May 15, June 30, August 1? Give us a date! We'll be happy! Any date, we want to know. But we're not going to know. What we can count on is that those who wait for the Lord, those who long for the Lord, those who look for the Lord, those who aspire to be part of God's kingdom shall renew their strength. They shall mount up with wings like eagles, they shall run and not be weary, they shall walk and not be faint. That should get us through any situation for any period of time. If God be for us who could be against us? Would you pray with me?

Almighty and ever-loving God, sometimes we begin to think that we are the center of the universe, that you should do everything to meet our demands. O heavenly Father, help us to gain a perspective, help us to see that you are the God and Creator of us all and that sometimes your ways are not knowable to us but yet we know that whether in crises or in calm you are that ever-present help in each of our lives. Help us indeed, O Lord, to lean on you, to abide in your love so that we can mount up like wings of Eagles, so we can run and not be weary, so that we can walk and not be faint. We pray this all in Jesus name and for his sake, Amen.

Preacher's note:

I've included Darren Utley's sermon here not only because it allows you to have the entire sermon series that he and I preached from the pulpit of Fairfield Presbyterian Church but also because I think he is a fine young preacher himself. While his style might be different than mine, I admire the discipline and intelligence he brings to his task as well as his heart for sharing the Kingdom with everyone.

Descending to Share the Story
Mark 9: 2-9

February 14, 2021

The Reverend Darren W. Utley

We have spent a number of weeks in this sermon series about God's creativity and the ways that God is continually is creating new life all around us — reconciling and remaking the world. We have been moving through the Christian season of Epiphany, as well, trying to allow the spirit to enlighten us to the ways of God's creative love among us. Today we come to the close of both the sermon series and the season of Epiphany. Around the corner in the Christian year is Ash Wednesday and the season of Lent. Our text this morning serves as both an epitome of epiphany with Jesus transfigured on the mountain and as we will see also serves as a perfect segue into the season of Lent.

2Six days later, Jesus took with him Peter and James and John, and led them up a high mountain apart, by themselves. And he was transfigured before them, 3and his clothes became dazzling white, such as no one[a] on earth could bleach them. 4And there appeared to them Elijah with Moses, who were talking with Jesus. 5Then Peter said to Jesus, "Rabbi, it is good for us to be here; let us make three dwellings,[b] one for you, one for Moses, and one for Elijah." 6He did not know what to say, for they were terrified. 7Then a cloud overshadowed them, and from the cloud there came a voice, "This is my Son, the Beloved;[c] listen to him!" 8Suddenly when they looked around, they saw no one with them any more, but only Jesus. 9As they were coming down the mountain, he ordered them to tell no one about what they had seen, until after the Son of Man had risen from the dead.

To return to the theme of God's creativity we see in this scene the creative power of God to do something unique that no one can imitate — clothes so dazzlingly bright like no one could bleach them. God's ability to give something new form, to remake the ordinary into something extraordinary. At the same time, it is utter uniqueness of this moment that makes it hard for us to understand. If we were there or if we had a beautiful painting of it then we could be moved to awe and wonder, but that's not what we get in this gospel. What we do get is the inspired story telling of Mark and the way he structures his gospel in order to help us understand what this scene is meant to create in us.

I want to focus on the voice of God from the cloud claiming Jesus as both son and beloved. This is the second time that God has spoken from the clouds in Mark's gospel. In the first chapter, after his baptism, the heavens are ripped open and the spirit descends and God speaks to Jesus directly, "You are my son, the beloved, with you I am well pleased. " That moment of epiphany is followed by Jesus trail in the wilderness for 40 days. The pattern on which our Lenten journey is shaped.

Here, six days after Jesus has foretold his death, been tried by Peter who he calls Satan, Jesus is transfigured before the three disciples and God speaks to all of them saying, "This is my son the Beloved, listen to him. " This last words that Mark has Jesus speak before this scene are directions for taking up our own crosses in order to follow Jesus.

One of the things that we are meant to learn from the first claim of sonship by a pleased Father in chapter one and through to this point in the text is what it looks like to have a son of God living among us. Mark hopes that we have been paying attention to all that Jesus has done and said… confronting and casting out evil spirits, healing minds and bodies, curing lepers, teaching compassion, sharing God's love, comforting the poor, crossing boundaries to embrace the outsider. By connecting these two scenes from the beginning and ending of the gospel Mark wants us to see that the glory of this moment is bound up with the struggle and striving of the healing, feedings, confrontations with principalities and powers both human and spiritual. This mountain top moment is an affirmation of everything Jesus has done and said… "This is my Son the Beloved, listen to him. "

This is why it makes perfect sense that we move from the brilliant glory of the birth of the Christ child through the wonders of epiphany back into the season of Lent. The season of following, taking up our cross, listening and learning from Jesus and following in his way. Of course, that does not make the work of taking up our cross any easier, and like Peter we would rather pitch our tent on the mountaintop and bask in the glorious light of God's glory. But like the disciples we are called to descend and follow Jesus into confrontation with the forces of evil —follow him to the cross.

Once more in Mark, Jesus is called the Son of God. It comes in one of the final scenes of the gospel when Jesus dies on the cross.

*Then Jesus gave a loud cry and breathed his last. **38**And the curtain of the temple was torn in two, from top to bottom. **39**Now when the centurion, who stood facing him, saw that in this way he breathed his last, he said, "Truly this man was God's Son!"*

There are a couple of things about the movement toward this final acclamation of Jesus' sonship that I think offer us inspiration for the Lenten journey.

First, we note at Jesus baptism that the heavens are torn open and the Spirit descends, then in our text this morning God simply speaks from the cloud, and at Jesus' death the curtain in the temple is torn in two. Mark is telling us that with the coming of Jesus any separation we might imagine between the realm of God and our world has been torn down, ripped asunder. From the heavenly veil created by God to the temple veil fashioned by human hands nothing stands in the way of God's Spirit, God's love moving among us, speaking to us, claiming us as beloved children.

And we have a mission. Notice that there is a movement from God speaking to Jesus, God speaking to Jesus and the disciples then to the recognition of the centurion. Mark has assured us of God's presence with us, and has shown us how Jesus commissions us to follow in his teaching, healing and helping.

The power of God to remake and recreate has descended on Jesus and he has shared it with us. God has filled us with the light of Christ so that we can confront the darkness of this world. Along the way there will be mountaintop moments of warmth and glory. And there will be times of sacrifice and struggle as we seek to cast away all that keeps us from following Christ fully. Mark wants us to see that often the mountaintop and the cross are connected. Even when we breath our last the breath of the spirit may be lighting the way for even our enemy to see the truth of Jesus Christ.

Remember that the veil is torn, the Lord is with us. Listen to the words and witness of Jesus, take up your cross and follow. God's creative love will remake and reform us so that our witness will bear fruit for the kingdom. Amen.

Change
Mark 1: 9-15

February 21, 2021

This is the first Sunday of Lent and Lent is, for us as Presbyterians, just one of those seasons that we not always sure of what to do with it. I grew up in a predominately Roman Catholic community and as I was growing up, you know my Catholic friends made all sorts of sacrifices for the season of Lent. They gave up candy or ice cream or whatever it might be. They made these offers of sacrifice "During Lent I will give up.... (whatever it may be.)"I never really caught on to that. I'd like to say that I gave up eating vegetable for Lent one year and never got back into it, but as Protestants we just didn't do that sort of thing. We didn't give up anything, we just went into the season of Lent. We might add, and as we're doing here with our Wednesday night Zoom prayer meeting, add an element of learning and devotion study to it - just a little extra discipline that we're adding to our season of Lent. That's the kind of thing that Presbyterians do, we love the Book, we're people of the Book and we'll discipline ourselves to spend more time in the Book. But we've just never really been all that comfortable with Lent. It's not one that we look forward to. I haven't had anybody come up and say to me, "I can't wait! It's almost Lent! "Hasn't happened.

Lent is so important for us to experience. It's so important for us to go through the season of Lent. And the theme that Darren and I will be walking all of us through this Lent is the theme of "The Power of Sacrifice. "Now I know we Presbyterians don't like the word sacrifice because immediately we think, "Uh Oh - the preacher is going to ask us for more money. "But that's not it. If only it were that easy, if only it were as easy as throwing an extra dollar in the offering plate on a Sunday morning. The sacrifice that we're talking about is the sacrifice of ourselves in the seeking out of who it is God has called us to be. So, we will go through some of the basics of the Christian faith and some of the basics of what this season of Lent is all about because in order to get to Easter, we have to understand more carefully, more closely who we are. It is, by its very nature, a season of introspection, of looking at ourselves, looking at who we are and comparing ourselves to who God calls us to be. And to see how far apart those two are. Because if we can understand who we are and how distant we are from whom God has called us to be, then we can understand all the more clearly what it is that Jesus Christ has done for us. The week we call Passion week or Holy week, what Good Friday and Maundy Thursday means for us and then, if we can understand that, then we can begin to understand what Easter means in our lives.

This morning I want us to go to the book of Mark. Now you all know that Mark is my favorite of the four gospels because Mark doesn't do a lot of frou-frou. Mark is straight forward, succinct, precise, and just cuts right to the chase. So, we're going to look in the first chapter of the Gospel according to Mark, the 9 - 15th verses there.

"At that time Jesus came from Nazareth in Galilee and was baptized by John in the Jordan. As Jesus was coming up out of the water, he saw heaven being torn open and the Spirit descending on him like a dove. And a voice came from heaven: "You are my Son, whom I love; with you I am well pleased. "At once the Spirit sent him out into the desert, and he was in the desert forty days, being tempted by Satan. He was with the wild animals, and angels attended him. After John was put in prison, Jesus went into Galilee proclaiming the good news of God. "The time has come," he said, "The kingdom of God is near. Repent and believe the good news! 'May God bless this a portion from his holy word.

Repent! Now there's a word you don't hear in a Presbyterian church too often. That has more of a Baptist ring to it, doesn't it? We don't like the word "repent", we just don't pay any attention to it. We ignore it, we don't use it, we don't even think about it but here it is that Jesus is beginning his earthly ministry and the first word he says to us is "Repent! The kingdom is at hand. The kingdom is near. "Now the word "repent" - if you go back to the Hebrew word "*shauv*" if I remember correctly, it literally means to do a 180 degree turn, to go in a whole different direction, to change how one is proceeding from point A now heading towards point B. Now, when you are reversing direction, how do you do that? If I'm heading this way (walking forward!) and I reverse direction, am I just going to do this? (Walking backward!) Probably not, because I'll trip and fall in no time. But if I'm going to reverse direction the first thing that I do is I change my perspective. I change the way that I am looking at things and I see where it is that I want to go and as my eyes have gone, my feet will follow. That's repentance. . . to change our perspective, to change what it is that we are looking for, what it is that we are searching after, what it is that we are setting as our primary focus in our lives. "Repent, for the kingdom of God is now. "It's here, it's at hand, it's near. It's translated a number of different ways but the implication of Jesus' words were that it's starting right now and that requires us to change our focus, to change our perspective, to change what it is that we are chasing after with our lives. So that it is a call for us to live our lives in a different way, in a different manner, to follow the way of Jesus Christ.

At his baptism, just that short time ago, the baptism which was the first acknowledgment particularly in the gospel of Mark, of the exceptional person of Jesus Christ. We hear a voice coming from heaven saying, "This is my Son, this is the one that I really love and in him I am pleased. I'm really proud of him. "Well that's an interesting statement to make because so far all that Jesus has done was get himself baptized. But, what Jesus has already done was taking on human form, "He did not consider his equality with God, something to be clung to, something to be grasped, something to be held on to, something to be hoarded but instead emptied himself up taking on human form and even with the willingness to go to the cross for you and for me. " (Preacher's paraphrase)

So, to follow Jesus Christ, to change our focus means that we go from living lives that are self-centered, living lives that are more interested in "what's in it for me" to living lives that are exemplified by the kind of love that Jesus showed in his life. All throughout his life and his ministry, there was always that core emphasis of loving others more than loving self. Jesus healed those who were hurting whether physically, spiritually, mentally, whatever it may be, he healed others. He always loved other people and he had a particular, exceptional, unconditional love for those, others who thought to be irredeemable. He loved the unlovable. He cared for those who were outcast, those who were cast aside by society. He went and he ate dinner with sinners, which was just a euphemism in those days for unacceptable people. He never thought about himself. He always thought about others.

There's an old saying, an old question actually: If you were arrested for being a Christian, would there be enough evidence to convict you? Does your life reflect your faith in Jesus Christ? A good number of years ago now, back up in Conklin, I did a funeral for a woman who was a member of the church there. After the funeral service, as people were shuffling out from the sanctuary, a fellow that I had never met before came up and shook my hand and says, "That was a good service Reverend. "I said, "Thank you. "He said, "You know, I worked alongside this woman for over 20 years. We shared an office. I never knew she was a Christian. I never knew that she went to church anywhere. "That conversation sticks with me all these many years later. It would be just a horrible way to be remembered. To be somebody that people didn't know was a Christian. Somebody whose life did not reflect the love of Jesus Christ. If we were arrested for being Christians, would there be enough evidence to convict us?

Now, I don't want you to get this wrong. I don't want you to think that I'm saying that we have to go out there and wear our Christian faith on our sleeves. I don't want you to think that I'm asking you to go out there like grab people and ask them if they know Jesus. That's not what I'm saying. It's not about proving to anyone your Christian faith, it's about that repentance. Where is your focus? Where is your heart? Where are your actions? Do our lives reflect the kind of love that Jesus exemplified in his life? Will people know that you are a Christian because of your selfless love, kindness and generosity?

There have been times when Debby and I have been together and we would meet somebody such as when we were traveling by train a number of years ago and had conversations with people over dinner in the dining car. I would get back to our room and Debby and I would talk and I'd say, "I bet my bottom dollar that that person is a Christian. "There was just something about the conversation, something about the way they treated us as strangers, that there was something about them that I could see the love of Christ flowing through them. No words were exchanged, no conversation was held about what church they went to or anything like that, but it would seem to me that person was a Christian by their lifestyle, by the manner that they dealt with us as strangers on a journey. That's what Jesus is calling us to do. To live our lives in such a way, that we are selfless, that our lives are focused on not what's best for me but on how might I show Christ's love to others, even to strangers, even to people who are 180 degrees different from us in every measurement. "Repent," Jesus said, "for the Kingdom of God starts here. "It starts with you, starts with me. The Kingdom of God is when we live our lives under the reign, the lordship of Jesus Christ. When we live our lives in such a way that people will see in us not ourselves, but Jesus Christ living through us. If we were arrested for being Christians, would we be convicted? Would you pray with me?

Our heavenly Father, to repent, it's not something that comes easily or naturally but help us, O Lord, to turn around, to focus our hearts and our lives upon the love that we have seen in Jesus Christ. To let that love flow in through us so that others around us might see and to know that the kingdom, the kingdom of your love is here. We pray this in Jesus' name, Amen.

Preacher's notes:

This appendix includes three sermons which were written by three very special people in my life. The first is by far the most meaningful to me. It was written by my Dad and preached on Father's Day 1995. That was the day he suffered his mortal stroke. He had his stroke at the 9:00 a. m. worship service at the Waymart (PA) Presbyterian Church. He refused to go to the hospital because he knew the good people of the Union Dale (PA) Presbyterian Church were waiting for him at their 11:00 a. m. worship service. My brother, John, drove him to that church and Dad wasn't able to lead the worship and john again stepped in to assist. Somehow, Dad was able to preach this sermon and John immediately took him to the hospital following that service. Dad died a little over a month later after a lifetime of service to the Church of Jesus Christ. We all agreed that Dad loved to proclaim the good news of Jesus Christ and this final sermon of his sums it up for us.

Robert Peak has been a true friend for more than 30 years. He is a shining example of what a Pastor/Preacher is. He has faithfully served the people of the First Presbyterian Church of Johnson City, NY for more than thirty years now. It is a small but strong church serving in a community which has been beset by economic downturns. Which churches all around it have closed their doors, they remain, under Robert's leadership, a shining light to their community. His sermon is an excellent example of how a Pastor, through the spoken Word, leads a congregation through a trying time.

Steve Chastain and I shared for a few years the leadership of the Conklin (NY) Presbyterian Church. I grew to love and admire Steve for his heart for the people and his love of Jesus Christ. Like Robert Peak, he now serves churches that are small in number but are faithful to their calling. Steve's understanding of the Scriptures and his love of his congregations shows through in the sermon which I have included here. His role as a Pastor/Preacher in this period of struggle is exemplary for us all.

Enjoy! ! And Grow! !

Go into All The World
Philemon 1-22

June 18, 1995

The Reverend Charles F. J. Starzer

Waymart Presbyterian Church and Union Dale Presbyterian Church, PA

Paul, a prisoner of Christ Jesus, and Timothy our brother, to Philemon our dear friend and co-worker, to Apphia our sister, to Archippus our fellow soldier, and to the church in your house: Grace to you and peace from God our Father and the Lord Jesus Christ. When I remember you in my prayers, I always thank my God because I hear of your love for all the saints and your faith toward the Lord Jesus. I pray that the sharing of your faith may become effective when you perceive all the good that we may do for Christ. I have indeed received much joy and encouragement from your love, because the hearts of the saints have been refreshed through you, my brother. For this reason, though I am bold enough in Christ to command you to do your duty, yet I would rather appeal to you on the basis of love—and I, Paul, do this as an old man, and now also as a prisoner of Christ Jesus. I am appealing to you for my child, Onesimus, whose father I have become during my imprisonment. Formerly he was useless to you, but now he is indeed useful both to you and to me. I am sending him, that is, my own heart, back to you. I wanted to keep him with me, so that he might be of service to me in your place during my imprisonment for the gospel; but I preferred to do nothing without your consent, in order that your good deed might be voluntary and not something forced. Perhaps this is the reason he was separated from you for a while, so that you might have him back forever, no longer as a slave but more than a slave, a beloved brother—especially to me but how much more to you, both in the flesh and in the Lord. So if you consider me your partner, welcome him as you would welcome me. If he has wronged you in any way, or owes you anything, charge that to my account. I, Paul, am writing this with my own hand: I will repay it. I say nothing about your owing me even your own self. Yes, brother, let me have this benefit from you in the Lord! Refresh my heart in Christ. Confident of your obedience, I am writing to you, knowing that you will do even more than I say.

One thing more—prepare a guest room for me, for I am hoping through your prayers to be restored to you.

As our Lord finished his ministry on the earth, one of his closing commandments was for his followers was to go into all the world with the Good News. I was reminded of this command as I learned of Dr. Billy Graham's illness and thought back over more than fifty years of his active reaching out to the thousands, if not millions, in the course of his ministry with the Gospel Message. With the detraction of others seeking to glorify themselves and bringing discredit on those who have given their lives to the truth. And going back to St. Paul and the disciples and the problems they had with those making a mockery of the Message of Salvation. Yet the strength of their message comes through and carries on.

They have done their job and Dr. Graham will continue to do his work as long as the Lord permits. But where does that leave us? As a pastor and a small group of Christians in this small corner of the world, as followers we too have to obey that command. Each one of us, you included, are commanded to go out into the world.

The Gospel message is one on one. If you followed the workings of the evangelical programs, there are prayer meetings and visitations, etc. Churches working together to reach out to individuals to come to the meetings long before those meetings take place. With all of the preaching and teaching it is one person reaching out to another with their lives.

St. Paul and Silas were arrested as recorded in the Book of Acts the 16th chapter, are placed in jail. Now they could have complained and raised all sorts of ruckus, instead they spent the time praying and singing. When their bonds were shattered, they made no attempt to escape; instead they took time out to give the jailer the message of life.

The lesson this morning begins with no complaint. Paul was a prisoner of Christ, not of the Roman government. Paul is writing to a fellow Christian, writing about a run-away slave. I have spoken on this passage a great number of times and each time I re-read it, I come across something a little different. The main idea here, has been to my thinking, the fact that here we have someone, a crook, I have an idea that some money might have been stolen and the fact that the slave was a runaway, both items were punishable by death. Paul is pleading for the life of this slave with a little side note that they would like to keep him for himself to be of some service but felt that he should go back to his master - even promising to make up for anything this slave might owe him. Take him back now as a brother in Christ (still a slave.)(As a passing note, we can say at this time that this slave later proved himself and was one of the early Bishops in the Christian Church.)

That would be my original thought, that here was a con, very worthless, - his very name meant "useless" - was now a great value. But, the important thing here is not only the conversion but the fact that slave must have seen something in the life of St. Paul to make him want to change. There must have been something in the life of Paul and Silas in an earlier prison that caused the Jailer to change his life and accept Christ as his Savior.

Down through the years I have heard a number of times from people outside the church that they do not go because someone turned them off. By the same token, there are many people who have accepted Christ because of someone's life. Without the prayers and the life of each one of us, those who follow us might never learn of God's love. Do not let it ever be said that you turned someone off to the truth because of your life.

Basic Construction
1 Corinthians 3: 1-17

The Rev. Robert Peak
First Presbyterian Church of Johnson City, NY

October 4, 2020

Have you ever tried to lay foundation after a building is already built? Have you ever heard of such a thing? No. Why? Because the foundation is necessary for the building to stand strong. Otherwise the wind and the rain, the snow and the ice begin to erode the earth beneath the building. And as the ground shifts beneath it, the building gets weaker and more prone to a catastrophic failure. A foundation provides stability.

We all know this, but something else about a foundation that may not be immediately apparent, is that it also dictates how the building is going to be built – where we put wings and doorways and load-bearing walls. The foundation shapes both the form and the function of the building. If we try to build outside the foundation or put too much building on a foundation, either we will put up a building that is in constant need of repair or one that will collapse under its own weight.

Laying the right foundation is important – no more than that, it is essential. Which is why Paul spent the first part of his letter to the Corinthians reminding them what is foundational to the Christian faith – what is essential.

We've been working our way through 1 Corinthians over the past two weeks and in some ways we have found Paul's needle stuck on the centrality of the Gospel.

When face to face with the physical evidence presented to us by the science community the temptation is to accommodate the Gospel to the scientific view. When presented with the doctrines of tolerance and relative truth and situational ethics coming out of the institutions of higher learning the temptation is to acquiesce, to hedge the Gospel in order to appear more tolerant and not so close-minded. When faced with the thinking of the world, we feel like we have to dress up the Gospel to make it more attractive.

But Paul argued that we don't have to spruce up the Gospel; we don't need to adorn it with flashing lights, bells and whistles. We simply need to put it out there in plain and simple language – it is the power of God unto salvation.

And last week we talked about why the Gospel seems so foolish to those who reject it – how what can seem so reasonable to us can be so unreasonable to the unbelieving. *(The week before I spoke about needing the plans/blueprints before building)*

After we have embraced the Gospel we forget that we didn't comprehend it because we are incredibly brilliant and its mysteries couldn't hide from our piercing intellects. We forget that we were once as dumb as those who just shake their heads and walk away, muttering about fairytales and how we should know better. So what's the difference? *(This was a bit of sarcasm)*

So essentially Paul is telling us in these first two chapters, embrace the foolishness of the Gospel! Grab hold of it, revel in it, invest yourself in it because it is the way of salvation. Don't let any slick-talking, promise-making huckster lead you away from the very simple story of the Gospel; Christ has died, Christ has risen, Christ will come again. That is where our hope lies, it is where life is found and it is the only message that can lead to the salvation of another.

So why do you think Paul is so intent on sounding like a broken record here? Why would he hammer so hard on the importance of the Gospel? In our text for this morning Paul provides the answer in two different analogies – the first one rooted in agriculture, the second grounded in construction.

Read I Corinthians 3:1-17

Now, let's imagine that I am just now starting the sermon and I look out at you and say, "Look, you bunch of babies you really need to grow up. You should be a lot further along in your faith journey, but here you are still struggling with just the basics. You guys are squabbling over things that really don't matter – who cares what color the carpet is? ! Who cares if you're democrat or republican? Aren't we supposed to be beyond that? Shouldn't our unity depend on something greater? "

That, in essence, is how Paul addresses the Corinthians in our text for this morning. You know what's really cool about what he says here?

Look at vv. 3-4. "You are still worldly. For since there is jealousy and quarreling among you, are you not worldly? Are you not acting like mere men? 4 For when one says, "I follow Paul," and another, "I follow Apollos," are you not mere men? "

Paul voices an expectation there that I think can slip right by us – a standard that we should be taking to heart. He calls the Corinthians "mere men," which by implication means we're to be more than merely human.

More than merely human? Yes, more than merely human. But how? How can we be more than merely human? **Paul's point is this – if we find ourselves trying to bring the world's ambitions, the world's hungers, the world's desires into the church, maybe we need to look at our relationship with Jesus. If our way of**

thinking, if our way of responding, if our way of acting still looks like the rest of the world – in other words, if we are not changing to become more like Jesus Christ – maybe we should think about spending a little more time with him. If we judge success and failure by the same broken standards the world uses – standards clouded by prejudices, fears, and cravings for love and power – maybe we need to do a gut check and see if Jesus really is our Lord or if we have been playing at faith the way children play house.

The reality is when we take up our cross and follow Jesus, we do become more than merely human. We become part of the new humanity – a new race of humankind with spirits that are no longer dead, but have been raised to new life in Christ. We have something the average person doesn't have – a living spirit in a restored relationship with the Creator God. And more than that, we have the Holy Spirit dwelling in us, sustaining us with life, enabling us to follow after Jesus Christ. We're no longer bound to sin – no longer a slave to the sin nature. We have a new master now, Jesus Christ, and our lives are meant to be reflect his – to become like his. Do you get that, how big that really is?

And the way Paul is speaking about this to the Corinthians, this is not a by and by expectation – a pie in the sky sort of thing. With the phrase "mere men" Paul makes it clear that conforming to the image of Christ is a here and now activity. Will it be completed in this life? No, but it should be happening as Paul writes in 2 Corinthians 3:17-18

Now the Lord is the Spirit, and where the Spirit of the Lord is, there is freedom. 18 And we, who with unveiled faces all reflect a the Lord's glory, are being transformed into his likeness with ever-increasing glory, which comes from the Lord, who is the Spirit.

I dwell here because the question that Paul asks the Corinthians is one we should be asking daily with every encounter we have with others. Do they see anything in us that shows that we are not merely human? The reality is we often use that as our excuse – when we allow our weakness to dominate our lives we console ourselves with "Well, I am only human." When we lash out in anger, when we lie to save ourselves embarrassment, when hesitate because we fear a loss of status, when we deal with others dishonestly because it will bring us financial gain, when we use company time for personal gratification our excuse is always, "Well, we're only human."

But asking the question, Paul says "We're supposed to be more." Are you merely human or are you a child of the King? Are you merely human or a co-heir with Christ? What would your friends, co-workers, neighbors and families say? Are you being transformed into his likeness with ever-increasing glory? Do a gut check this week.

Paul has written some pretty inflammatory things to the Corinthians; not very endearing. But remember, Paul is a man under inspiration here and so even this has a purpose. It serves to point out the foolishness the Corinthians were displaying by pitting against each other based on human teacher.

What, after all, is Apollos? And what is Paul? Only servants, through whom you came to believe—as the Lord has assigned to each his task. <u>vs6 I planted the seed, Apollos watered it, but God made it grow.</u>

Come on! Paul is saying, "You guys are focusing on the wrong thing! It's not the "farm-hand" that matters, but the farmer. Apollos and I are working for the same thing, can't you see that?" Paul uses the image of a farm where he and Apollos labor as hired hands in the employ of God to give the Corinthians a big picture view of how God works through the church. This isn't about personal gain or glory – Apollos and I are not in competition.

To drive the point home Paul then switches to a construction image – with the Corinthian Church being the building and he the wise master builder. The wise label is important here – remember, the Corinthians are enamored by all things touted as wisdom. And he displays that wisdom magnificently, "By the grace God has given me, I laid a foundation as an expert builder, and someone else is building on it. But each one should be careful how he builds. 11 For no one can lay any foundation other than the one already laid, which is Jesus Christ. "

You know, if you go to build a house, the guy you contract to do it will most likely not be the guy who builds every part of it. He may be a great framer, but will subcontract the exterior, the drywall, the electrical and plumbing. That's the image that Paul is drawing for us – he's the primary contractor for the Corinthian church who knows what it takes to build a structure that will last. He knows that what he starts, others will finish, but in order for them to do their jobs he has to lay a solid foundation – one that won't crack under the pressure of the elements or the weight of the house itself. He also knows that the foundation he lays will dictate both the form and the function of the building. For the church, there is only one foundation that can be laid – Jesus Christ. Any other foundation will ultimately lead to a catastrophic failure.

Parts based on sermon by Christopher Lanham delivered on Jul 19, 2010

The Midnight Wedding
Matthew 25:1-13 (NLT)

The Rev. Dr. Steve Chastain
Conklin Ave. First Baptist Church, Binghamton, NY
& Community Baptist Church, Port Dickinson, NY

Aug. 9, 2020

Outline:
The Bridegroom Was Delayed
The Faithful Get Drowsy
Those Ready Are Feasted

Good Morning!

We've come to the final installment of our series on this incredible parable that Jesus tells about the ten bridesmaids that we've been considering for the last couple of weeks. One of the most important principles to remember whenever you are reading the Bible is to carefully take note of the context of whatever Scripture passage you are studying.

Because Jesus doesn't just tell this parable about the wise and foolish bridesmaids without a back-story. And if you recall, the context of this passage is that Jesus has come into the city of Jerusalem during the final week of His life and everyone is talking about Him, wondering if He will call for an insurrection, an uprising. All the common folks have decided that Jesus must be the long awaited

Messiah, especially after He called Lazarus back to life, after Lazarus had been dead and buried for four days.

But here's the problem. You can believe that Jesus is the Messiah, the Son of God, and still want to use Him for your own agendas. We do it all the time. This is exactly why so many of us get angry with God when we don't receive the answers to our prayers that we want. This is why so many find themselves angry and enraged more about politics than they care about their spiritual health.

And these folks in the first century were no different. They wanted to use Jesus to give them an understanding of what to expect in the future. They wanted Him to prepare them for what lay ahead. Which is just another way of saying, they supported Jesus in hopes that they could use His insider connections to avoid suffering.

And that's not a relationship. They wanted Jesus to be their political/logistical deliverer, not their God, and certainly not their Friend.

So - Jesus told them this parable that we're about to read. And if you've missed the earlier two messages that I've shared on this profound story, I encourage you to look back over the Facebook posts on either church website because there's a lot more here than I can ever exhaust in three sermons.

But for now, let's read this story one last time and pray over it before we digest it again together.

Read Matt. 25:1-13 (NLT)
Pray.

I'm doing my first wedding of this year this week, after most of them were cancelled or postponed. And I was thinking about how marriage ceremonies have been impacted during the Age of Covid and I saw this cartoon and thought you might enjoy seeing it.

(Cartoon picture of bride, groom, and minister on three separate zoom meeting screens)
If you can't read the caption underneath the minister it says, *"Mary, do you accept John as your lawfully wedded husband? If so, signify by pressing 'Enter' on your keyboard. If not, press 'escape.'"*

In spite of all our modern day ceremonial challenges, this parable illustrating a wedding is an image that Jesus uses again and again to try and help His listeners understand what the Kingdom of God is like.

So I just wanted to conclude this series with a simple summary of some principles that I think Jesus wants us to remember while we watch the world around us changing so dramatically. The original readers of Matthew's account were also involved in a traumatic time of world history.

And when we are living in this kind of worldwide uncertainty it does put everyone on edge. We all want to avoid unnecessary suffering if possible and so it IS wise to plan ahead, to follow the science and the politics and to try to prepare for seasons of struggle.

But there is something more majestic in this story that Jesus is trying to get all of His listeners to remember about the big picture of the Christian life. I've entitled today's sermon, The Midnight Wedding because that's such a key emphasis in the narrative.

First century weddings in the region of Palestine generally did take place after dark in the cool of the day, because when the people of that agrarian age worked outside in the heat farming all day they got tired and sleepy after dark just like we do. And so when Jesus says in verse 5 that **"the Bridegroom was delayed,"** which I have as our first point, Jesus is signifying something unusual that we need to take note of.

I believe that He wants all of us who long to somehow shortcut the difficulties of life by having insider knowledge or just simple lazy bones, Jesus wants all of us to remember that really living the Christian life with Him, being a follower of Jesus is going to feel like He is being delayed.

These bridesmaids were all drowsy and sleepy Jesus said at the end of verse 5. The foolish AND the wise ones all reached the point where they were tired and unable to remain awake. And I've mentioned before how this could be symbolic of physical death or our own bodily weariness or both, but the principle remains the same.

We will not be able to use God, or figure out a timeline of Jesus' return in order to somehow avoid struggle, suffering, or patient waiting. This is a significant principle of following the Bridegroom and believing in Him. Faithfully, patiently preparing and awaiting His arrival.

One of the interesting aspects of this marriage procession, the mini parade which the Bridegroom would have taken to get to the house of His Bride, that I've mentioned before, is that normally the men in the wedding party would take the longest route possible through the village. And the purpose of this extended journey was to involve the entire village in the joy of the wedding festivities.

So don't miss this aspect of the **delay** in the arrival of the Bridegroom. His entire bridal party is having to be patient because the Bridegroom is traveling throughout the entire village that was known to Him; going past every home and down every street, in order to proclaim His joy and to invite everyone to come out and acknowledge Him and share in His joy with their love and affirmation.

Jesus is saying, when you think about the end of this age as we know it, think about this picture of a wedding celebration. Think about the desire in the heart of the Bridegroom to have *everyone* participate with Him in the celebration. This Bridegroom is delayed because He wants all His neighbors in the village to share in His joy.

That's so important to remember when you are a member of the wedding party waiting patiently for the Groom's arrival. And when Jesus said these women got **drowsy**, He wanted His listeners to understand this is an important dynamic of our spiritual journey that we all should be aware of.

During this year of pandemic, it has really helped me to believe that somehow the whole world is being more prepared for the arrival of Jesus; that somehow the Good News of the Kingdom of Love and Forgiveness and Healing is becoming even more precious as it travels down every highway and avenue and side street and backcountry lane.

I don't want things to "get back to normal" if it means going back to the way things have always been in this world of institutional religion. I want there to be a growing awareness of the fact that we are one day closer to the wedding feast of the Lamb and the Bridegroom is out there in the streets, moving through our world, announcing His wedding, proclaiming His Love and preparing the way for everyone in the village to enter that celebration. That's the kind of Messiah I can follow.

That's the kind of Savior I can trust. A Bridegroom Who won't leave anyone behind; Who announces to every single citizen from east to west, from rich to poor, that you are His neighbor and that He is getting married and that you are an especially selected guest of honor at His wedding feast.

The bad news is that we can become drowsy and sleepy and lazy and we can get ourselves into a place of real problems when we are not awake and aware; when we stop believing in the heart of our Bridegroom travelling around in the dark after midnight.

When Jesus tells another version of this parable in Luke 14, He tells it from the different perspective of the Father of the Bridegroom. And when the Father sends out all the invitations for His Son's wedding feast, people begin to make all kinds of excuses.

Jesus describes their responses in Luke 14:18-20 (NLT)

But they all began making excuses. One said, 'I have just bought a field and must inspect it. Please excuse me.' 19 Another said, 'I have just bought five pairs of oxen, and I want to try them out. Please excuse me.' 20 Another said, 'I just got married, so I can't come.'

Did you notice how genuinely important each of those responsibilities are? Land purchases, livestock investment, and family priorities. All essential responsibilities in a farming culture.

But this is what can happen. Our worldly *duties* can cause us to forget to prioritize our spiritual *health*. Both are important, but one is much more important than the other. Because if you are not spiritually healthy you cannot attend to any of your other life responsibilities without trying to draw life from them, because your heart is hungry. And when your soul is not nourished you cannot bring life to your work, your home, or your relationships.

And when that is the case, you will miss the celebration.

The Good News is quietly mentioned, almost as an afterthought by Jesus, back in our primary passage in Matthew 25 verse 10, where Jesus said:

"But while (the foolish bridesmaids) were gone to (attend to all these earthly chores), the bridegroom came. Then those who were ready went in with him to the marriage feast..."

Those Ready Are Feasted is the way I put this idea in the final point of the outline.

That's the Good News which Jesus wants to plant like a small seed in the midst of all our fear and uncertainty about the present and the future. When we are willing to honestly look at the things that are misdirecting our attention from the feast; you realize - that's exactly what evil wants to do. Evil just tries to distract us from the most important things.

Like a bad magic trick misdirects your attention, evil wants you to glance at something flashy, like politics or quick fix solutions that the world offers so you won't look at what's really going on in your soul spiritually.

Jesus is saying, don't be fooled by the idea that if you are informed enough, or smart enough, or get the right political party in power, or invest your money in the right places, or even find the right medical vaccine that you can somehow ensure the future that you want. If you are attending to these important duties in life out of a fear that makes you believe you have to provide for yourself, then you are in danger of missing the celebration.

This is why I keep referencing that verse in Luke 8:18 where Jesus said, **"Pay attention to how you hear! To those who listen to My teaching, more understanding will be given. But for those who are not listening, even what they think they understand will be taken away from them."**

If we listen through the filter of fear instead of faith, then even what understanding we think we have can be lost.

But (!) people, if you are listening in faith that the celebration is being arranged with you already a member of the wedding party; if you believe that the Bridegroom is taking every side street and dusty dirt road in order to find you; if you believe that the Father of the Bridegroom has sent the Holy Spirit of God into your soul to make your heart come alive to receive and believe and feast on this Good News, then even more understanding of His love will be given.

Jesus said in Mark 13:32, *"However, no one knows the day or hour when these things will happen, not even the angels in heaven or the Son himself. Only the Father knows. 33 And since you don't know when that time will come, be on guard! Stay alert!"*

And here's where we need to end our time in this parable with what Jesus said in Luke 12,

"Be dressed for service and keep your lamps burning, 36 as though you were waiting for your master to return from the wedding feast. Then you will be ready to open the door and let him in the moment he arrives and knocks. 37 The servants who are ready and waiting for his return will be rewarded. I tell you the truth, <u>he himself will seat them, put on an apron, and serve them as they sit and eat</u>! 38 He may come in the middle of the night or just before dawn. But whenever he comes, he will reward the servants who are ready."

Let's pray.

www.ingramcontent.com/pod-product-compliance
Lightning Source LLC
Chambersburg PA
CBHW072006110526
44592CB00012B/1215